What is Happiness?

First published in Korea as 법륜 스님의 행복
by Munhakdongne publishing Co. in 2016

First published in Great Britain in 2025 by

Greenfinch
An imprint of Quercus Editions Limited
Carmelite House
50 Victoria Embankment
London EC4Y 0DZ

An Hachette UK company
The authorised representative in the EEA is Hachette Ireland,
8 Castlecourt Centre, Dublin 15, D15 XTP3, Ireland (email: info@hbgi.ie)

Copyright © 2016 Ven. Pomnyun Sunim

English translation copyright © 2025 Jungto International Translation Team

The moral right of Ven. Pomnyun Sunim to be identified as the
author of this work has been asserted in accordance with
the Copyright, Designs and Patents Act, 1988.

All rights reserved. No part of this publication may be reproduced
or transmitted in any form or by any means, electronic or mechanical,
including photocopy, recording, or any information storage and
retrieval system, without permission in writing from the publisher.

A CIP catalogue record for this book is available
from the British Library

HB ISBN 978-1-52944-128-4

Quercus Editions Limited hereby exclude all liability to the extent
permitted by law for any errors or omissions in this book and for any
loss, damage or expense (whether direct or indirect) suffered by a
third party relying on any information contained in this book.

10 9 8 7 6 5

Typeset by seagulls.net
Cover design by Steve Leard
Cover illustration by MaSeol (recreated by Amber Badger)
Printed and bound in Great Britain by Clays Ltd, Elcograf S.p.A.

Papers used by Greenfinch are from well-managed forests
and other responsible sources.

What is Happiness?

A Monk's Guide to Living a Happy Life

Ven. Pomnyun Sunim

Translated from the Korean by
Jungto International Translation Team

greenfinch

I am the one who creates my own happiness.

I am the one who creates my own unhappiness.

Nobody except me creates my happiness
or my unhappiness.

PREFACE

Everyone Has the Right to Be Happy

In my Dharma talks, I often ask people: 'Are you happy?'. Few answer 'yes'.

Many people worry and suffer because of personal issues, emotional damage, relationship conflicts, frustration, stress caused by lifestyle and social pressures, or anxiety about the future. Many changes and events occur throughout our lives, and often things don't turn out the way we think we want them to. We want to be loved, but we may end up getting hurt. People we care about may treat us poorly or even betray us. Nothing happens without a reason, but the reason is not God's will or even punishment for a sin committed in a previous life. Often, we must accept that we simply do not know the reasons why things turn out the way they do. But if we could identify where our suffering comes from, we could easily find a way to overcome it and free ourselves from suffering entirely.

A big part of our unhappiness comes from our inability to let go. Imagine, for example, that a stranger swears at us as we pass in the street. This is much the same as someone handing us a bag of rotten rubbish as they walk by. For some reason, instead of just putting it down and walking away, we hold the bag tightly, even rummaging through its contents, for the rest of our lives. We say to ourselves, 'That person swore at me, slighted me and harmed me.' We wonder why they did that, whether we did something to provoke such behaviour. We wonder whether we deserved it or may be angry we allowed such an insult.

When we cling to such negative feelings, we can never access the path to happiness. If a person actually tried to hand us a real bag of rotten rubbish, we would certainly refuse to take it. If we were to accept it by mistake, we would most likely be disgusted and immediately throw it away. Unfortunately, often the results of insults or other types of harm are negative feelings we continue to hold deep in our hearts. These feelings make it difficult for us to be truly happy no matter how hard we may try.

Happiness faces many obstacles, such as unfulfilled desires, bad habits, living in an unjust society and even our own thoughts. If our suffering arises from negative thoughts, we should try to change this habit of negative thinking. If we suffer from a relationship that has gone sour, we should examine the cause of the failure and take steps to correct the situation. If we believe that our social system is the problem, we should first try to adapt to the current system. If we are certain that society is, in fact, the actual source of our problems, we should find ways to make some real change in the society we live in. However, most of us just continue to complain without making any real effort to change our situation. As a result, the world around us doesn't change and neither do our circumstances, and we continue to be miserable.

Everyone born into this world has the right to be happy.

For more than thirty years, I have mainly focused on how individuals should cultivate positive attitudes through their own practice, as a way of affecting change for those who do not recognize or exercise this right to be happy, and who therefore live in a state of suffering. In this book, I will also discuss social change, another positive action we can make towards happiness. Ultimately, our happiness will be whole and complete only when our individual, internal attitudes (the seeds of happiness and fulfillment) and our external social conditions (the soil in which these seeds are sown) are cultivated together.

What is Happiness?

Attaining individual happiness and working towards a decent and just society are not two separate, distinct aspirations. The lone efforts of a single individual are unlikely to make significant improvements to the world. Better external conditions alone are unlikely to make any individual happy. Happiness and unhappiness are the combined result of a person's attitudes and general wellbeing as well as their environment and surroundings. We must look within and reflect on ourselves before blaming others for our problems and any sense of discontent. We must also take responsibility for improving our own surroundings and situation as much as we are able. Ultimately, both will benefit us. We must also accept that no matter how ardently and sincerely we commit to leading a good life, each of us is bound to suffer when things go wrong in the world around us. Complacent thoughts like 'As long as I am not being harmed, it's all right,' or 'That couldn't possibly happen to me,' will not protect us.

To take our first steps on the path to happiness, we must commit to accepting responsibility for our own lives and our own happiness. Each of us is an insignificant entity, less than a speck of dust floating in space, but when we become the masters of our own lives, we can change ourselves and our world.

When we commit to changing the world for the better, for everyone's benefit, rather than just aiming to lead a good life for personal gain, we simultaneously take steps towards both our own contentment and the improvement of the wider world. The possibility of happiness becomes a reality, rather than a dream. Being helpful to the world and to others around us increases our own personal happiness.

This book is based on the conversations shared in my Dharma Q&A sessions, and it tells the story of people who escape from the suffering they are experiencing to become free and happy. The content of this book is not an abstract or philosophical explanation – it contains specific conversations between me and the questioner. These conversations explore problems that occur in real life, and they demonstrate the process of finding realistic solutions to these everyday problems. My hope is that this book will be a guide towards happiness for those of you searching for hope, those feeling drained by life and living, those who have suffered pain because of relationships or other circumstances, and all suffering needlessly while trying to make sense of this seemingly irrational world.

Ven. Pomnyun Sunim

CONTENTS

Part 01 /
Why Doesn't Life Go According to Plan?

Choice and Self-Contradiction ⋯ 3
Between the Real and the Ideal ⋯ 10
Escaping the 'False Sense of Self' Prison ⋯ 17
The Secret to Happiness ⋯ 26
Setting a Goal After Letting Go of Greed ⋯ 34
Time Lag Between Cause and Effect ⋯ 41

Part 02 /
Habits Form Feelings

Freedom From Likes and Dislikes ⋯ 51
Anger, the Inner Fuse That We Ignite Ourselves ⋯ 57
Neither Suppressing Nor Venting Anger: A Third Path ⋯ 64
When Feeling Indignant About Not Having Retorted to
    What Someone Said ⋯ 71
Transforming Existing Wounds into Life Assets ⋯ 76
Regret Results From Clinging onto Past Mistakes ⋯ 81

Anxiety Is the Result of an Obsession with the Future ⋯ 87
Superiority Complexes and Inferiority Complexes Come From the Same Place ⋯ 94
Feelings Arise, Stay, Change and Disappear ⋯ 100
Formed Habits Can Be Changed ⋯ 105

Part 03 /
Living with People Who Hold Different Opinions

All Conflicts Stem From Relationships ⋯ 113
Good or Bad? ⋯ 118
No One Has Everything in This World ⋯ 122
Conditions for a Happy Marriage ⋯ 131
Are You Living a Truly Good Life or Just a Life That Looks Good to Others? ⋯ 135
The Boss Who Teaches You the Middle Way ⋯ 141
Most Relationships Are Based on Selfishness ⋯ 146
Give-and-Take is a Transaction, Not Love ⋯ 155

Life Will Feel Empty if You Live with a Sense of
    Responsibility ⋯ 159
Dependence: the Seed of Resentment ⋯ 165
Stop Interfering in Other People's Lives ⋯ 170
All the Trees Together Make a Forest ⋯ 176

Part 04 /
We Need to Revise the Definition of Happiness

What Is True Success? ⋯ 183
Do Not Build Your Happiness on Other People's
    Misfortune ⋯ 188
Desire Is Like a Burning Log ⋯ 196
Three Levels of Want: Need, Desire and Greed ⋯ 202
The Individual is the Seed and Society is the Field ⋯ 211
When Two Hunters Catch Three Rabbits ⋯ 217
Establish Yourself as a Good Example Before Criticizing
    Others ⋯ 222
How to Be Happy and Benefit Others at the Same Time ⋯ 230

Part 05 /
Practice Being Happier Today Than Yesterday

Letting Go of Judgments ··· 241
Insightfulness, the Wisdom of Seeing the Whole ··· 247
The Merit of Comforting Others ··· 254
Different Levels of Love ··· 262
Happiness Lies in Fun and Rewarding Activities ··· 267
How to Organize Your Time to Live Happily ··· 273
We Can Choose to Be Happy at Any Moment ··· 279

About the Author ··· 283

Part 01

Why Doesn't Life Go According to Plan?

People waiting at a bus stop will each have different thoughts going through their heads. One may be feeling hurried and anxious. They may be checking the time, wondering, 'Why isn't the bus here already?' Another may be blaming someone else for their current anxiety, thinking 'I would have been on time for the earlier bus if I hadn't had to answer the door while I was getting ready this morning.' A third person may be consumed by a completely different worry, thinking, 'This bus is taking ages to arrive, it's bound to be crowded by now.'

Such negative thinking is habitual for some, but others manage to maintain a positive attitude. Positive people likely wait patiently for the same bus. They may be thinking to themselves, 'I can't make the bus arrive any sooner by fretting and worrying about it.' When they finally do catch the bus only to find it uncomfortably crowded, they are more likely to think, 'Even though I can't sit down, thank goodness I was able to get on the bus.'

A continuous stream of such moments flows through the lives of many of us. Unfortunately, we waste much of our precious time and energy feeling anxious and fretful in the moment, then regretting it later.

When we wrestle with difficulties in this way, we are failing to live in the present because we are focused on wishing for things to get better in the future. Even when everything is going fine, we become anxious that something bad may happen to disrupt our peace or good fortune. We may fail to enjoy even a moment of true happiness as time races past us.

Choice and Self-Contradiction

Throughout our lives, we make the choices we think best based on the information available to us. In hindsight, we often come to realize that our choices did not lead to the best possible outcomes. We hope that marrying will make us happy, but marriage might cause unhappiness. You might have a child, expecting a resulting sense of fulfilment, but the realities of parenting might lead you to envy others who do not have children to take care of. A person may start a business hoping to make a good amount of money, but instead end up struggling with debt. We often feel regretful and miserable when things don't turn out the way we hoped and intended. We are left longing for control over our lives rather than feeling as though we are simply swept along by the currents in the world. Are we actually in control of our own lives?

Once there was a man who hoped to attain enlightenment, so he left his home, his assets, his work and position in society, and his loved ones in order to become a monk. After years of practice at a temple, he came to believe that it would be impossible to attain enlightenment if he continued to live within a community of monks. He felt he didn't have enough time to practice because he had to do chores, cook meals, and perform the various tasks that go hand in hand with communal living. He thought it would be better to leave and go alone, deep into the mountains, so that he could devote himself entirely to his practice, uninterrupted and fully focused.

So the man left the other monks and travelled alone, far into the mountains, to a spot 10 kilometres from the nearest village. There he built a thatched cottage to live in. When he needed food, he walked down to the village. But rather than finding the freedom to practice, the man discovered he actually now spent more time working than he had at the monastery. The cottage required frequent repairs, and the man often needed to make the 20-km (12½-mile) round trip to source food from the village. Furthermore, walking such long distances wore out his shoes, and he needed to make new ones more often than he had before. Living alone like this, he found that he had much less time than before to devote to his practice.

To make matters worse, the man soon became ill. He consulted a doctor, who told him that his illness was caused by malnutrition and if he was to regain his strength, he should drink milk every day. But walking to the village and back for milk every single day was too time-consuming, so the man bought a pair of goats.

Keeping the goats saved him the trouble of making a daily trip to the village, but the man found that the goats led to even more chores. He had to tether the goats to prevent them from wandering off, and he had to supply enough food for them. The goats provided the milk he needed for his health, but tending to their needs left him with even less time to practice. In order to solve this new problem, he hired a goatherd. But the goatherd required payment.

Previously, during his alms round, the man had only to request enough to provide food for himself. But now he needed more, as he needed to provide for the goatherd as well. So his alms round took up much more time. He knew he couldn't continue this way.

He thought that perhaps it might be better for him to marry, so he would have someone to help with everything that needed to be done. And so, before too long, he married. Now his wife took care of the goats, so he didn't have to pay the goatherd anymore. And his wife took care of their home, so he didn't need to spend time on housework. Now, finally, he could concentrate on his practice.

Then his new wife became pregnant.

And so, the man who left his home, his work and his loved ones to become a monk in the hope of attaining enlightenment ended up getting married, having children, and scraping together a living to provide for his wife and children.

Hearing this man's story, you might think him foolish. But most of us live our lives the same way. We think that our choices are good at the time we make them, but looking back we can see that those decisions were shortsighted, and perhaps that in making them we forgot our ultimate goal and purpose. If a person marries, they should live accordingly. If a person leaves home in search of enlightenment, they should also live accordingly. If we were to keep such a clear perspective on life, we would suffer less, but we are often tempted by the promise of easy solutions when we face problems. Suffering from the rigours and responsibilities of daily life, we might decide instead to seek enlightenment. Having devoted our lives to the process of attaining enlightenment, we might realize that this too brings its own difficulties. We may start to envy a layman's life and find ourselves thinking, 'This practice is too hard.'

We may also make foolish decisions, like the monk in the story who lost track of his bigger goal as he looked for solutions to more immediate problems. Faced with this reality, we have two options. The first is to disregard our ultimate goals and live instead according to the situation in which we find ourselves. There is really nothing wrong with this approach. The other option is to return to the path towards our ultimate goal the moment we realize that we have deviated from it.

Out of habit, people may say things such as, 'I will be happy when I have more money,' or 'I will be happy when I find a life partner.' But when the time comes that they make more money or they settle down with a life partner, many find that they are still not happy. Before having children, many think they will be happier when they have a child. But then, once they have a child, it is hard work and they become convinced that they will be happier when their child starts school, when they will have more time. Next, they think they'll be happy when their child passes their exams, or is offered a place at a particular university. When their child leaves for university, the person still continues to postpone their own happiness, believing that they will be happy when their child gets a good job, then when their child gets married, then when they have a grandchild, or when their grandchild grows up and becomes independent. Throughout their lives, people keep changing the conditions they think they need to be happy. As a result, they may die without ever having tasted happiness.

Wealth, work, fame, family, friends or the lack of them, are not the root cause of suffering, nor are they the ingredients for happiness. Sometimes, we believe that these things will make us happy; at other times, we think they bring us pain and suffering. If we bounce back and forth between these two extremes, we will never be free of suffering.

If you're married, instead of being dissatisfied and worrying, it would be better to think, 'I have a spouse, a home, a job. I have nothing in the world to envy. My life is the best.' If we accept our life as it is, we will become content. Rather than resolving to change the way we think about our situation starting tomorrow, or perhaps the day after tomorrow, we have to learn to be happy here and now.

In life, there is no single answer that will always be the right choice. We live as we choose to. But we hesitate when making choices because we don't want to be responsible for unwanted consequences. We cannot know what the future will hold, just as we cannot say for certain that life is ultimately good or bad. We have choices, and inevitably the responsibilities that result from the choices we make. Accepting responsibility for our own choices means accepting the consequences. If we truly accept the consequences of our actions, we won't be miserable or resentful, no matter the outcome.

Between the Real and the Ideal

Sometimes we may feel that we are being left behind, or missing out, while others fulfil their dreams, enjoy success, have fun, and live their lives to the fullest. Our inner conflict is amplified when our hopes and dreams have to be sacrificed because of particular circumstances.

A person in their thirties might complain that they had to give up on their dreams in order to make a living, and facing this reality might make them very unhappy. 'If I had the means,' they might grumble, 'I would return to studying so I could pursue my dream career, but now that I'm married and have a child, I can't afford to quit my job and follow that dream.' They would likely end up wondering if abandoning their dream is the right thing to do.

Many of us believe that we'd be happy if we had the job our skills were best suited to. Aptitude is vitally important to some jobs, but less so for others.

It was my dream to become a scientist, and I thought that I had a talent for it. I never even imagined that I would become a monk. I have endured much torment and inner conflict over the years, living as a Buddhist monk rather than as a scientist.

However, since leaving home at 16 to live as a monk, I've tried to apply the principles of scientific thinking to my life in a new way. I didn't believe in the baseless precepts of religion, so I distanced myself from them. I thought hard about the question, 'What can I do to help people more easily understand the Buddha's teachings?' This is why, in my Dharma talks, I try to deliver the Buddha's teachings coherently and logically. No matter what kind of work you do, it will always be affected by your personal beliefs and strengths.

However, when you believe you have an aptitude for science, you may come to believe that you need to have a job related to science in order to find your work fulfilling. This is a fixed notion. You can't be sure that your aptitude will only fit the specific jobs you happen to know about or have in mind. Instead, when you commit and apply yourself, you will find that you can use your talents and abilities to perform well in any job.

I often tell young people who are looking for work to do what they really want to do. I tell them to do something for which they have a passion, something that makes them excited. Young job seekers should think carefully about the true meaning of these words. They should explore the kind of work that will suit them personally, rather than pursuing professions that seem to promise money, social status, power or security. If someone discovers a job that they really find appealing and believe they would be good at, they should explore it. They should pursue such opportunities even if it seems unlikely they will make a lot of money doing so. They should not waste time worrying about whether or not such opportunities are 'good' jobs. The occupations that we typically label as 'good' are not necessarily 'good' for everyone. One should not blindly follow a career path just because the majority of people recommend it as 'good'. Rather, you should seek work that feels 'good' to you.

That said, it is not necessary to torment yourself trying to work out what your passion is, or what you would like to devote your life to, if you are not sure. Some people have a passion for one particular thing, and some do not. Perhaps being without a particular passion enables you to be content with whatever work you find. This would allow you greater freedom. Those on the highest level of enlightenment live this way –

cooking when cooking is required, doing laundry when laundry is needed, delivering a lecture when a lecture needs to be given, and doing farm work when farm work has to be done.

Greater freedom is possible when we do not insist on a rigid or strict approach. Most people cannot attain such freedom, so they try to focus on at least one thing and try to do it well. So, right now, you don't really have to worry about not wanting to do anything with passion or liking anything in particular.

Moreover, you shouldn't despair if you are not currently able to do the one thing that you believe you want to do. Perhaps you would love to study design, for example, but your current situation means this is not possible. Instead you could try to incorporate the ideas and principles of design into your current work, instead of agonising over not being in a position to pursue design as an independent career at the moment.

Let's say you become a monk. Wouldn't you still have the opportunity to practice design? You could incorporate your interest into your lifestyle and your practice, learning more about the design of monks' robes, exploring the layout of the monastery garden, or studying the modernized temple designs created to preserve the structures' traditional beauty. The kind of job you do is not really the most important thing – it is your attention and the interests and skills you bring to your job that matter. If you work on whatever happens to come your way, you will be able to find your particular skills and make good use of your talent.

Ignoring your present reality while searching for your dream, and pursuing only future happiness, is like trying to build a castle in the air. But focusing only on making a living in the present will leave you without hope for the future. People agonize over whether to pursue their ideals or focus on their present circumstances. However, the relationship between future ideals and present reality does not need to create tension. Ackonweldge both. Plant your feet firmly in reality, while you raise eyes towards your ideals.

In the late 1980s, I opened a Dharma centre. My aspiration was to break away from the common practice of seeking good fortune, and instead focus on studying the Buddha's original teachings and attaining enlightenment. Prior to opening the centre myself, I tried to apply this aspiration to an existing Korean Buddhist temple – my attempt led to conflicts. At that temple, it was customary to pray for blessings and perform ancestral rites in the hope of receiving good fortune, but I refused to participate. People complained about me to the abbot. They said, 'If this monk continues to refuse these prayers and rituals, we will lose all our lay Buddhists.'

As a result, I had no choice but to leave the temple and open a small Dharma centre of my own, in which I started to spread the Buddha's teaching. Did many people recognize my good intentions and come to the centre? No, they didn't.

At first, I handed out leaflets that read, 'I have opened a Dharma centre. Please, come to study the Buddha's teachings.' About ten people came to the centre, but after a disappointed look around the tiny centre, they left and never came back. Still, I didn't give up and kept handing out leaflets.

I prepared a three-month Buddhist lecture programme and invited a famous monk to the opening ceremony. Five people came that day, but after the first lecture, only one remained. After planning a three-month course of study and receiving such poor attendance, I'm sure most people would have cancelled the programme. I delivered the lecture series to the one remaining student for the entire three months.

After the first lecture series ended, the one person who had attended brought several acquaintances to the Dharma centre. I handed out more leaflets; ten more people came and five of them stayed. I gave the three-month lecture programme to these new students. This is how the Dharma centre began and slowly grew, to become the Jungto Society of today.

I was penniless at the time, so how was I able to keep the Dharma centre open? On the days I didn't give lectures, I worked part-time at a local academy as a maths instructor, and I used the money I earned there to cover the expenses of running the centre. I continued doing this for the next four years and only stopped once the Dharma centre was finally able to support itself financially.

If I had given up because the situation felt difficult, I wouldn't have been able to take the path I wanted to follow. Even when we are sure of our dream for the future, we may sometimes doubt whether we are on the right path. At times like these, we must work hard in the present, while simultaneously considering how things might be different in ten years' time. We should think carefully about the best way to face each day's challenges. Simply waiting passively will not bring about a positive future.

We build a reality from our dreams for the future by engaging with and overcoming challenges arising along the way.

Escaping the 'False Sense of Self' Prison

People complain about their lives not going their way or the world not working in their favour. Are they satisfied with themselves? No. It seems that most people who are not happy with the direction of their lives are not satisfied with themselves either. Even those who appear to have relatively few problems, and seem to live in enviable circumstances, often feel this ongoing sense of dissatisfaction. Why is that? When we are not satisfied with ourselves, the reason is often not that we're not good enough, but rather than we set overly high expectations for ourselves. The dissatisfaction we experience results from falling short of these high expectations.

We feel that we're not good enough. We think we are, or should be, exceptional people. Stuck within this perception of ourselves, we feel certain we must be superior to others. But when the facts of our lives and lifestyles do not fit with this perception, when reality does not justify our belief that we must be better than others, we become frustrated. Thus, we oscillate between blaming others for our frustration and blaming ourselves for our own perceived incompetence and failures.

A man once asked me for advice. He had spent much of his life resentful that he had been born into a poor family but at the same time felt guilty for entertaining such thoughts. 'All my life,' he said, 'I've blamed my family's poverty on the incompetence of my parents. Once I began to practice, I stopped blaming my parents. Instead I regretted my resentment, and I have since repented a great deal. Now I feel unhappy about myself and feel depressed and guilty about my previous resentment. I blame myself. How can I move past my regret in order to accept myself as I am?'

If you have repented about previously resenting your parents, it is fine tell yourself that your parents have given you a lot and that it was foolish to resent them. But you should go no further. If you blame yourself for having resented your parents, you're just shifting the target of your resentment from your parents to yourself. That is not the solution.

Just as blaming your parents is not the attitude of a practitioner, neither is clinging to your regrettable past thoughts or behaviour. Continuously berating yourself for your actions will not obliterate them, or make you feel better. Instead, if you continue to blame yourself, you will become despondent. If these feelings worsen, you may even fall into a depression.

Depression is like a deep swamp. Once you are seized by a certain thought, it will engulf you quickly, and it will feel utterly real. At such times, shake your head, and consciously work to free yourself from the quagmire of such ideas. If you feel depressed while sitting, stand up and move around to change your mood. Take a bath, go for a walk, stretch your body, or complete some small tasks around your home or garden. Shake yourself out of that state of mind, so those depressing thoughts cannot take hold again.

We tend to fall into the trap of only believing we have made progress if we are able to reach the lofty standards our egos set for us. But this expectation does not benefit us. If you think that way, feeling satisfied with yourself becomes impossible. Happiness begins with accepting yourself as you are, acknowledging your current state and finding a way to be positive about it.

If you fall down, you are the one falling. If you get angry, you are the one getting angry. If we think of ourselves as the kind of person who doesn't stumble or doesn't lose our temper, it is painful to accept that we do. Since we cling to a self-image that we have formed, we become displeased. We are so full of our false sense of self that we come to feel ashamed of our real selves.

Your real self is neither good nor bad, but if your self-image seems better to you than your real self, then you'll feel you are not good enough. If your self-image seems worse than your real self, you'll feel that you are someone special.

When your self-image is too high, you will find it difficult to tolerate your real self. As a result, you may blame yourself for failing to live up to the false image you have created. You can be mentally healthy only when your self-image corresponds to your real self, when you understand the reality of yourself and accept it. This is why mentally healthy people do not despair, even in the face of difficulties.

When we think, 'I don't seem to know much about this problem. I'll study it and work out how to overcome it,' we can accept and think positively about ourselves and make a little more effort to change. But if you have a self-image that is much better than your real self, you can't satisfy yourself no matter how hard you try. In the end, you will despair and think, 'I am useless.' In short, the level of your happiness varies greatly depending on how you see yourself.

What happens if you believe that you will be able to run 100 metres in 13 seconds, when in reality, it may take you 20 seconds? Running the 100 metres in 20 seconds might not be a problem, but if you have decided you should be able to do it in 13 seconds and find that you can't no matter how hard you try, you will blame yourself and feel that you are failing.

Feeling insecure or inferior is an inevitable result of delusions of grandeur. Your conceit and false perceptions about your life as overly significant will in fact make you miserable. There is no special meaning to existence. As people learn this, some begin to question whether there is any reason to live, or they say, 'Isn't it sad to live in this world if existence has no meaning?'

All beings, including human beings, have no special meaning. Meaning is simply conjured by human consciousness. Concepts such as 'valuable' and 'worthless', 'virtuous' and 'evil', 'good' and 'bad', heaven and hell, the Buddha and God, are all value judgements created by human consciousness to try and make sense of the world and to try and regulate the way we should live.

Just as the caterpillar spins a cocoon then locks itself away inside, so humans imprison themselves within concepts of their own creation. Charcoal and diamonds, both made of carbon, have no intrinsic value, yet people assign value to them. When the weather is so cold that you could freeze to death, charcoal will be much more useful than diamonds. People may become miserable if they believe they should shine like diamonds, but if they change their views and aspire to be useful, as charcoal can be, they may lead worthwhile lives and make a difference to others.

The same is true when people evaluate others. If someone who doesn't know anything about me comes to my Dharma talk without any expectations, they might walk away thinking, 'Wow, he's great.' Perhaps they expected my ability might be about 50, but after listening to my Dharma talk, they decided that my ability is in fact closer to 100, so their evaluation is very positive. Another person might attend my Dharma talk, having heard that I am a renowned monk, and they may expect my ability to be 150. After listening to my talk and deciding it doesn't meet their high expectations, they may think, 'There was nothing special in his talk. I don't see what all the fuss was about.' My ability is still 100, but the listener with low expectations will be more satisfied, whereas the one who came with high expectations will be less satisfied.

Sometimes, when we look at someone else's behaviour we wonder, 'Why on earth would they do that?'. We feel frustrated or confused about this other person, because their actions do not fit the specific image we have created for them. Based on our own standards, their behaviour might seem unsatisfactory or misguided. But the truth is that the standard against which we have been measuring that person is nothing more than our own illusion.

You might believe your spouse to be a certain type of person or assume that your child should act a certain way. Your family may therefore disappoint you because you are measuring them against an arbitrary framework that you have created and that you now require them to fit into. Just as we should not expect too much of ourselves, we should not expect too much of others. We should instead accept others as they are.

The fact is that you are not all that special, and neither are others. If you feel dissatisfied with others because they don't meet your standards, the problem is not theirs but yours. The problem is in fact your level of expectation.

You need escape the prison created by your false sense of self. Instead of making a resolution to be a certain way, become aware that regrets and self-blaming come from an illusory sense of self. This awareness is the first step to freeing yourself.

Just become aware of yourself, that's all. Don't hate yourself. If you hate yourself for making mistakes, you have foolishly defined yourself as someone who must not ever make any mistakes. Forgive yourself for making mistakes, just as you should forgive others for making mistakes.

Resolve instead that when you fall, you will get right back up and continue on your way. Rather than blame yourself for falling, try not to fall again but at the same time acknowledge that it may happen. Starting today, you can practice accepting yourself as you are. Be kind and generous to yourself. Then, you will gradually and naturally become kinder to and more accepting of others.

All beings in the world are neither perfect nor imperfect. Because we prefer to think that we are special, we paradoxically come to feel that we are small and worthless. Human beings, animals, grass and stones all just exist. Humans are animals, not all that different from squirrels and rabbits. Human consciousness is just a little different to that of other animals. As far as we know, squirrels and rabbits don't suffer due to their thoughts, so it seems wrong for humans to suffer because of the thought that life is hard. Imagine how shackled humans must feel if they envy a bird's ability to fly.

We are just like the grass and the ants. We are both insignificant and also precious. Once we truly understand and accept this, we can live peacefully without caring about what others think of us, and without interfering in the lives of others.

The Secret to Happiness

Once a lay Buddhist said to me, 'I have made donations to temples countless times, but this has not brought me any blessings. If it was guaranteed that donating $1 would return $100 in equivalent value to me, I would donate so much more.'

Desiring $100 in return for donating $1 at a temple is no different from gambling in a casino. Even without praying for material rewards, the things that people ask for in prayers offered to the Buddha at a big temple are sometimes just as absurd. Many people wish to gain a great deal with minimal effort. For instance, they pray for their child, who has poor grades and does not work hard in school, to be admitted to a good college. Or they pray for good health without wanting to exercise and eat a healthy diet.

If you pray this way, you are bound to invite misfortune. The desire to work only a little but to receive a lot is the mindset of a thief. This outcome requires that someone else must sacrifice what would have otherwise been due to them. For example, should your child who does not work hard and achieves only poor grades be admitted to a good college, someone else's child who has better grades may be denied admittance to that college.

It makes sense that such prayers should go unanswered, but people do not consider whether their request is unreasonable. Instead, they end up blaming the Buddha or God when they do not get what they want.

People usually pray for things they believe it would be difficult to achieve on their own, which makes it very unlikely that their prayers will be answered. As a result, their lives are filled with more pain, or at least disappointment, than joy.

Of course it would be pleasant if everything always went our way, but in reality, it doesn't. The belief that we just have to want something badly enough for it to happen is delusional and greedy. When something we want to happen doesn't, we then have a choice about whether to be unhappy, whether to cry and cling to our thoughts of what we want, or whether to move on and to live happily despite what has happened or not happened.

Must our lives be miserable if what we hope for doesn't happen? No. We suffer not because what we wish for doesn't happen, but because we believe that it should. If we can free ourselves from this way of thinking everything will be just fine, whether our wishes are fulfilled or not.

Even if we work hard to achieve what we want, it is no guarantee that things will always turn out the way we had hoped or expected. The result of our work is influenced to some degree by our own efforts, but also by the circumstances that surround us. When we understand this, we can avoid such deep disappointment on the occasions we don't succeed in gaining the results we want.

Enduring mistakes and even despair can actually make us stronger. When plants keep growing without being trimmed, they may grow leggy, fail to bear fruit, and are easily broken. When they survive pruning, or severe weather, plants may grow stronger and develop more successfully.

Whether what we want comes true or not, we can experience happiness during the process of working toward it. Most of us think that we can be happy and free only when everything turns out the way we want it to, once we actually achieve our goals – but often this is not possible. Sometimes, external circumstances make it possible for things to go our way, and other times, they make it unlikely. If our own happiness is permanently dependent on external conditions or circumstances, we can never be completely happy. Still, we cling to the desire that things should turn out the way we want, so naturally, we are sometimes unhappy.

Consider a farmer who spends an entire evening preparing to spray the crops in his fields early the next morning. Spraying is not effective on rainy days, so the farmer prays to the Buddha before he goes to sleep: 'Dear Lord Buddha, I plan to spray my crops tomorrow, so please don't let it rain.' Waking up to rain the next morning, the farmer complains, 'I had planned to spray pesticide today. The weather has been fine all week, and today of all days, it rains! Obviously it is no use praying to the Buddha.'

He is annoyed, but after a while, he begins to feel better and decides that since there isn't anything he can do about the rain, he will spend the following day planting pepper seedlings. Before going to sleep, he prays to the Buddha again: 'Dear Lord Buddha, now that it is raining, let it continue to rain tomorrow.'

He wakes up the following morning to find that the weather has cleared and once more becomes angry. 'What is going on with this weather? It's sunny when I want it to rain, and it rains when I want it to be sunny. How can I work if the weather is going to be so unpredictable? This is becoming impossible.'

If the farmer continues this way, failing to act and blaming the weather, he will inevitably ruin his crops. Likewise, blaming other people and circumstances – 'I can't be happy because of my child,' or 'I can't be happy because of my husband,' or 'I can't be happy because of my boss' – will ruin one's life.

What kind of attitude would benefit the farmer the most? At night, he should go to sleep peacefully. If the weather is favourable when he wakes up after a good night's sleep, he can prepare to spray his crops. If rain is drizzling instead, he could plant the pepper seedlings. If the rain is torrential, he should take a break, reminding himself that he has been working very hard lately and it would be beneficial to relax and spend the day resting.

It will be difficult for a farmer to do his job if he can't let go of his fixed expectations and wants –

he must be flexible. And so it is with our lives. Our environment changes constantly. If we are to avoid living in a constant state of suffering, we must let go of our expectations and desires about how things should be. Otherwise our happiness will be controlled by the unpredictable changes in our environment. If we set the conditions for our happiness in advance, and then insist on them, our prospects for happiness will drift away. If we let go of our insistence on everything going our way, and deal wisely with the circumstances as they are, happiness will naturally follow.

Despite this obvious truth, people demand to know the special secret to obtaining happiness without letting go of their insistence on obtaining it. Why? Because rather than letting go of high expectations, they continuously crave more. People want so many things, and unfortunately it is true that people often believe they will get what they want more quickly if they do things a certain way, according to a specific plan they have in mind.

Imagine a person is holding a firebrand, a burning piece of wood which represents their expectations and desires, in their left hand. They scream that it is hot, that it is searing their skin. I would tell that person something like, 'If it is so hot, let go of it.'

This person might ask me, 'How can I let go of it? Tell me how.'

Is this person asking because they truly don't know how to physically let go of the firebrand? Not really. They say that they want to let it drop, but actually, they don't want to let go, and so they continue to ask me how it is possible to drop it. There is only one answer I can give: 'Just let go.' They will ask again: 'How can I just let go?'

This person will say that Buddhism is very difficult and unrealistic, and they may complain that instead of teaching them how to let go of the burning stick, I just keep telling them to let it go. This problem can't be solved because they want someone else to fix their problem for them while they are avoiding acknowledging that they are the one gripping onto it. So, I'm forced to tell them to move the firebrand to their right hand instead.

Their expression brightens, and they say, 'You should have told me about this terrific solution earlier!' But will they be able to hold it in their right hand? No, not for long. It is still on fire. Soon, they will cry out that their right hand is now burning. They're holding onto it, not because they don't know how to let it go, but because they don't really want to. Unable to let go of attachment to the firebrand, this person continues to hold it while screaming in pain. Moving the firebrand from the left hand to the right and back again satisfies two purposes: It momentarily relieves the burning sensation and allows the person to continue to hold onto the firebrand. This may seem like a solution of sorts, but fundamentally it will not free the person from suffering.

Most people don't want to let go of what is burning them. When I tell them, 'Just drop it,' they tell me that this is not realistic, or not possible. When I tell them, 'So shift it to your other hand,' they agree, saying, 'What a good idea.' But in the end, they will simply experience the same burning sensation all over again. Swapping the firebrand they are holding from one hand to the other is only a temporary solution. To be happy, you have to let go as soon as you feel pain. Even knowing this, you may still occasionally suffer because you've developed the habit of holding on. Those who understand that they just need to let go do not suffer for very long. They only suffer momentarily when they become attached to something, but since they know they simply must let go, their suffering is short-lived. They know what to do. These are wise people who have learned and changed.

Setting a Goal After Letting Go of Greed

A doctor once asked me for advice. He wanted to give up his difficult and exhausting job in medicine and relocate far away. 'When I first began working as a doctor,' he said, 'I thought it was my vocation because I found it rewarding to treat sick people. Many people think highly of doctors, and the job pays a good salary. However, I find that I am barely able to put up with the work each day. I'm afraid of making a mistake, scared of medical accidents, and working is no longer fun for me. So I want to give up my practice and move abroad. But it's difficult for me to decide what to do because my daughter is only four years old.'

Buddhism instructs people to let go of greed, but people mistakenly think that letting go means avoiding all of the suffering in their lives.

So, what is the difference between letting go and evading reality? The biggest difference lies in the resulting consequences. When we let go, the same problem doesn't keep repeating, but when we act to simply evade reality, it does. If a man drinks every night to forget the pain of a breakup, he may momentarily escape from his pain, but when he sobers up, he'll feel it again. If, however, he lets go of his attachment to his former partner and instead thinks, 'Thank you for the time you spent with me. I understand that we have now parted ways and I wish you well. Goodbye,' he will no longer suffer. Letting go solves a problem; evading reality does not.

If a person doesn't have a good relationship with their parents and keeps avoiding their calls, the conflict they have with them (and therefore the suffering that accompanies it) will continue. By letting go of resistance to answering their parents' calls, the suffering will disappear. Willingly answering the calls from their parents will result in the calls no longer feeling like a burden. Even when it seems that a problem has been diminished or even solved by letting go of our attachment, the problem may occasionally recur. This happens when our minds once again begin to dwell on the problem. However, since we have already let go of the attachment, we are more easily able to overcome the problem. When instead we evade a problem by suppressing our feelings, it will grow worse over time. We may repress our feelings once, twice, three times, but eventually we will explode with anger, or grief, or sadness. When a problem occurs, it's better to face it head-on and solve it honestly and with courage, rather than trying to evade it.

If the doctor who asked me for advice leaves his job and moves to another country, he may feel relieved and peaceful at first. But fear or anxiety leading to the unresolved problem is likely to reoccur anytime, anywhere, and in any form.

In life, we find ourselves involved in four types of situations: The first is when we want to do something, and we can do it. The second is when we want to do something, but we cannot do it. The third is when we don't want to do something, and we don't have to do it. The fourth is when we don't want to do something, but we have to do it.

In the first situation, it is easy to just go ahead and do it. In the third situation, we can simply avoid what we don't want to do. Thus, we can live approximately half our lives in exactly the way we want to. The problem is that we also find ourselves in the second and fourth situations, in which we can't do something we want to, or we have to do something we don't want to do. If we follow our desires in either of these two situations, we are likely to bring misfortune upon ourselves. To avoid this outcome, we have to release our desire to act, or to avoid acting. If it is something we have to get done, we must let go of our aversion and take care of it.

Letting go of the desire to do something, which we experience as craving, or not wanting to do something, which we experience as aversion is, in Buddhism, referred to as 'letting go of greed' or 'emptying the mind.' People ask, 'How can I let go of greed in these fiercely competitive times?' They may likewise say, 'I let go of my greed, so my mind is at ease. But now I am concerned about feeling aimless and apathetic.'

Eating food when you are hungry is not greed. Sleeping when you are tired is not greed. Wearing warm clothes and seeking warmth when you are cold is not greed. Greed is continuing to eat even when you're full. Greed is not sharing your food with others when they are hungry. Wanting wealth or power is not, in itself, greed. Greed is not defined by the things you want, be they large or small. Greed is the desire for that which stands in contradiction.

For example, greed means wanting to avoid repaying a debt after borrowing money or wanting to withdraw a large sum of money without saving. Greed is the desire to be admitted to a good college without studying. Greed is the futile desire for things to go your way when it is not possible.

We suffer when the things we want don't come to fruition. The cause of this suffering is greed. That is why Buddhism teaches us to let go of greed and replace it with something else: aspiration.

What, then, is the difference between greed and aspiration? If you feel distressed when things don't go your way, you're being greedy. If you put in 30 per cent of the necessary effort but want the results only efforts of 100 per cent would achieve, your desire will not be realized. When you're being greedy, wanting a great outcome despite investing only minimal effort will make you feel miserable. Greed, rather than motivating or helping you, will hinder you from achieving your goal.

Those who have aspirations, and who make the necessary effort to achieve their goals, do not feel distressed or disappointed even if they fail. Instead, they look for other ways to achieve their goals. When a child is learning how to ride a bike, they never succeed right away; first they have to practice, over and over again. If a child becomes annoyed after falling once or twice, they may complain that there is something wrong with the bike or blame themselves for their clumsiness. This is greed based on the desire for an easy outcome with minimal effort. In order to learn how to ride a bike, they have to go through the process of falling repeatedly. If the child doesn't give up and continues to try despite falling down, we can say that the child has an aspiration to ride a bike. Wanting to ride a bike and trying until one succeeds is not greed.

Whether your aspiration is great or small, if you try hard to achieve it, your ability will grow. Even if you fail, you will develop the power and the capability to eventually succeed. If you try harder to achieve your goal, despite encountering obstacles, you have an aspiration. You can continue to work toward your goal, saying, 'It seems I have run into another obstacle, I will try a new strategy to overcome it.'

A person who has encountered an obstacle to achieving their aspiration examines it, analyses the likely effectiveness of potential solutions and tries again. If they eventually realize that they will not be able to achieve their goal after all, they will cease trying without regret no matter how much effort they have put in. They will not feel disappointed, regret their decision to try, or experience despair.

Ultimately, letting go of greed does not mean that you should not strive to be successful. If there is something you really want to achieve, of course you should try your best to attain it. When you make the effort to achieve your aspiration, life will be more enjoyable, and you will be more energized. Then, you will be more likely to achieve further success.

Time Lag Between Cause and Effect

One day, one of the Buddha's disciples asked, 'Lord Buddha, the Brahmans say that even if a person has committed bad deeds during his life, if a Brahman prays for them and makes an offering to the gods, that person will be forgiven and will go to heaven. Is that true?'

The Buddha picked up a stone and threw it into a nearby pond. Then he asked the disciple, 'If the Brahmans pray for the stone to float up to the surface, would the stone float up to the surface?'

Upon hearing the Buddha's question, the disciple realized how foolish his question was. It's not only one of nature's principles, but a case of simple logic that one who performs good deeds receives good consequences, and one who commits evil deeds receives bad consequences, just as a heavy stone will sink in water while oil is lighter than water and so floats on its surface. In Buddhism, this is called the Law of Causality.

We sometimes wonder whether the Law of Causality really applies to our lives. It seems that although we may have made every effort to live well, misfortune still befalls us, while those who have done many bad things seem to lead happy lives. It seems quite untrue that doing good deeds will be rewarded, while doing harm will be punished.

The Buddha said, 'A man cannot escape the consequences of his actions, whether he hides in the remotest mountains or the deepest sea.' It doesn't seem to be true in daily life, but if we look very carefully, we learn that the Law of Causality does hold.

For example, parents may feel that raising a child is just too difficult. They might even become irritated and angry with their child, not realizing the psychological damage their actions will have on their child. The consequences of their harmful actions do not always manifest themselves immediately, so it may be hard to relate the cause to the effect. But although the consequences may not appear right away, they certainly will show up eventually. The result of the parents' actions may not appear in the child until ten years later. At that point, the parents may feel that the consequences appeared with no reason.

Some consequences appear immediately, some appear after a few days, and others do not appear until years have passed. Some consequences will appear within our own lifetime, and some appear much later, in the lives of our descendants. There are times when we ourselves receive the consequences of our parents' or our ancestors' deeds.

There is a time lag between a cause and its effect. We see this in nature. The shortest day of the year, the winter solstice, is around December 22nd in the Northern Hemisphere. It seems logical that this should also be the coldest day of the year, but the coldest day of the year is actually sometime in late January or early February, about a month later. The longest day of the year in the Northern Hemisphere is around June 22nd, but the hottest days of the year are usually in late July and early August. The reason for this is that it still takes some time for the earth to warm up or cool down following the longest or shortest days.

In the same way, there is a time lag between a deed and its consequence. If we experience unwanted consequences even though we perform good deeds, the reason is that we are actually experiencing the effects of the bad deeds we have already committed, whereas the consequences of our good deeds have yet to manifest themselves in our lives. If we start practicing today, will everything suddenly start to go well immediately? Most likely not. Things may even get worse. This is not because we started to practice, but because we've done bad deeds in the past, for which the consequences are now appearing.

Many people don't know this principle, so when bad things occur in their lives despite their daily practice, they give up and stop practicing. This is like despairing of spring ever arriving when the weather grows colder after the winter solstice because of an expectation that the weather would warm up right away.

It is greedy to expect your situation or experience to improve immediately after we start to practice. If we continue to practice for a hundred days, without expecting anything, we will come to learn some truths about ourselves:

I am a little stubborn.

I get irritated easily.

I am impatient.

I complain a lot.

I have a strong sense of right and wrong.

When we start to understand a little bit about ourselves through practice, we will continue to practice every day, even though no one tells us we must. If we continue to practice for a thousand days, others may notice some changes in us and tell us that they can see we have changed.

The day we set an aspiration to begin practice can be compared to the winter solstice. The day we get to know a little about our karma through practice is like the start of spring, which is about a hundred days after the winter solstice. After a thousand days of practice, people may begin to tell us that we have changed, a point which can be compared to the peak of spring, when flowers are blooming everywhere. Just as we do not feel it is springtime until we notice the flowers beginning to bloom, others will not recognize the change in us until we've practiced for at least three years, even though we ourselves will feel that we have changed for the better long before that.

Obviously, if people received negative consequences immediately after doing something bad, occurrences of bad deeds would be drastically reduced. But the consequences don't usually appear right away, so people are tempted to do bad things thinking perhaps they will get away with them. Likewise, because we don't see the benefits of good deeds right away, we may not feel encouraged and motivated to continue doing them. This is why it can be easy to do bad things and difficult to do good things. But we must remember that, over time, the consequences of bad deeds cannot be avoided, and the rewards for good deeds are bound to appear. Although happy consequences do result from good deeds, they don't often appear in the form and at the time we want them to. We cannot control them. They arrive in their own time.

Thus, you shouldn't assume you have avoided negative consequences of your bad actions just because nothing has happened yet. Consequences are like debts, and the debt collector will be showing up sometime, whether sooner or later.

Remember there will be a time lag between your deeds and their consequences. You must not expect a positive, rewarding outcome to immediately follow a good deed. When you experience difficulties, accept them all as inevitable negative consequences for previous misdeeds.

When you do something positive or generous to help others, it is best to consider these actions as repayments of outstanding debts rather than an accumulation of merit. When we face difficult situations, we can easily overcome them by thinking, 'I must have a lot of debts, so now I am just making a contribution towards paying them back.'

We must perform good deeds without assuming that they will benefit us. Over time, these efforts will reap good results. These results are not random gifts from the universe. They are the consequences of the good deeds we have performed previously.

Part 02

Habits Form Feelings

When and how do sensations arise? They arise the instant our sensory organs (which mediate sight, hearing, smell, taste, touch or thought) meet their respective objects, just as a spark is produced when steel strikes flint. Sensations may be sorted into three different types according to our reactions: pleasant, unpleasant and neutral. These sensations result in either craving or aversion.

What, then, makes different people respond so differently to the same situation? The smell of soybean paste stew makes some people drool in anticipation, while others may grimace with revulsion. Those who have attended church since they were young feel uneasy about entering a Dharma centre, because their karma produces an unpleasant response to the new and unfamiliar surroundings. Similarly, those who have attended Buddhist temples since they were young may view Christian communal prayers as strange. But neither the church nor the temple is the actual source of these feelings. Individual responses are different because each person's karma is different.

The empty winter field looks desolate after the harvest, but when spring arrives, and the weather gets warm, green shoots sprout again. The fact that green shoots sprout teaches us that although we weren't able to see anything in the field, there were in fact seeds living under the soil.

Our minds are the same. Though not visible on the outside, everyone has their own individual karma, which responds to external stimuli. The karma ingrained in our bodies and minds creates sensations in response to external stimuli, such as colours, smells and sounds.

Freedom from Likes and Dislikes

When our six sense organs (the six roots in Buddhism: eyes, ears, nose, tongue, body and mind) come into contact with external conditions, we experience all kinds of emotions: joy, sadness, fear, loneliness, etc. We experience heaven when we like or love someone or something; we experience hell when we hate or resent someone or something. How do the emotions that make us feel happy or unhappy arise?

An emotion arises instantly, just like the spark generated by steel striking flint. If you were to see a stranger dying in the street, you would feel unsettled or upset even though you didn't know that person. You might feel sad. If you knew that the death had been caused by violence or some other injustice, you might feel scared or angry.

Because our emotions arise instantly in response to external stimuli, we mistakenly believe that we are born with them, and therefore conclude that they can't be changed because they are an inherent part of us. We shouldn't fixate on this idea and consider our emotions absolute. There is no objective substance to our likes and dislikes.

We might feel happy when we look at a flower. When we look at a rose and find it beautiful, we immediately feel good. This kind of feeling doesn't have any negative effects because we don't expect the rose to like us in return. We feel that the flower is beautiful, and that is all there is to it.

On the other hand, your heart pounds when you gaze at someone with whom you are infatuated. But you're also likely wondering whether that person shares your feelings. You may even be worrying, 'Does she like me as much as I like her?' or 'How can I make him like me back?'

Since you have these thoughts, and want the other person to like you, you feel confused, and your heart pounds. Your pounding heart may be a sign of fear that the person might not reciprocate your feelings, or anxiety about trying to control the situation. But no matter how strongly you feel you want the other person to like you, you cannot force this to happen. It's an illusion to think that if you adore someone, the object of your affection will feel the same about you. It is one thing for you to like someone, but it is a totally separate and unrelated thing for that person to like you in return. So, when your heart pounds in the presence of someone you like, recognize that you are most likely thinking, 'I want them to like me' rather than just 'I like them.'

A woman once asked me for advice, saying that there was someone at work whom she didn't like, but the problem was that her face made her feelings clear. 'I tend to draw a clear line between what I like and what I don't like,' she said, 'and I consider it part of my personality. However, frankly expressing my feelings at work hasn't helped me. Should I change?'

Everybody has likes and dislikes. You don't have to hide these feelings to be a good person. There is nothing wrong with expressing your likes and dislikes. However, you should understand that if you are allowing your feelings to push you around, you will become imprisoned by them, and this will be detrimental to you.

Our likes and dislikes result from our karma, that is, karmic consciousness. Consider the person who drools over the smell of soybean paste stew but feels nauseous at the smell of curry cooking. The latter response may be simply a resistance to something not previously experienced and, thus, unfamiliar. A certain stimulus does not produce the same exact feelings in everyone, regardless of whether each person finds something pleasant or unpleasant.

Feeling hungry when smelling soybean paste stew or feeling disgusted by the smell of curry are responses that arise from our karmic consciousness. We tend to think that our positive or negative reactions relate to something inherent to the object itself, just like we may believe that the scent of bean paste stew is itself delicious, while that of curry itself is inherently disgusting.

To two different people, the exact same colour may look completely different depending on their individual perceptions of colour, or the tint of the lenses they are wearing. In this way, you are the one who determines your likes and dislikes. If you really know that feelings of attraction and aversion originate from within you, you will realize that arguing about likes and dislikes is pointless. Understanding this means you are less likely to be overwhelmed or carried away by feelings that arise within you, even when you are powerless do anything to prevent them from happening.

If there is a person who thinks differently from you or who has a different point of view, there is no need for you to either try to get to know them or to avoid them. But you shouldn't try to change them to suit you, either. You just need to accept that they are as they are.

Each of us lives according to our karma. Something that doesn't make any sense to you might make perfect sense to someone else. When dealing with people in your life, accepting them as they are is the way to attain peace. You will be better able to accept and understand others if you consider, 'How on earth could I manage to change someone else's personality when I can't even change my own?' By adopting this perspective, you will find it easier to live or work with people with whom you feel you may not be compatible.

Until now, you have suffered and complained because you thought that your way was the only correct way. You probably thought that you had to live among those you love and had to distance yourself from those you hate. But think how much more free your life would be if you did not insist on your own likes and dislikes.

If you enjoy kimchi and steamed rice, you can just eat them. Suppressing your desire to eat what you like is not practice. It's also fine for you to refrain from eating something you don't like. You might, however, find yourself living abroad in a foreign country where you cannot easily find your favourite foods. If you don't eat because you don't have access to foods you like, your health will deteriorate. But your health will also deteriorate if you eat too much of the foods you like – you will gain unhealthy weight, or you'll develop a stomach ache, which is also harmful. Therefore, there are times when you must simply eat foods that are not your favourite, because you need to eat. There are also times when you shouldn't eat something, or shouldn't eat a great quantity of it, even though you enjoy it.

If we like something, we believe that we must have it. And if we don't like something, we believe that we must get rid of it or avoid it. We experience unhappiness because we find ourselves in situations where we can't get what we would like to have, or we can't get rid of or avoid something we don't like. In these situations, we endure suffering.

If you are in a situation where you either have to separate yourself from someone you like or have to spend time with someone you don't like, don't let your likes and dislikes entrap you. Simply do what must be done. In this way, you will find more freedom in your life.

Anger, the Inner Fuse That We Ignite Ourselves

Following anger, we are often left feeling stressed and regretful. After expressing anger, we may feel ashamed that we were not able to control our emotions, or we may feel remorse that we have hurt someone. Why is it that we can't withhold our anger even though we know it will bring such undesirable results?

We become angry when we believe that we are right and someone else is wrong, but they will not understand or admit that. We feel that we are so right that others appear to be completely in the wrong. Such feelings lie deep in our subconscious. They don't surface easily, but they may explode suddenly when we're with those who are closest to us, such as family members. After exploding in anger, we often say something like, 'I just saw red,' 'I completely lost my temper,' or 'I'm not sure why that made me so furious.'

Such statements signify that emotion is a habitual response arising from the subconsciousness.

But those who think differently might respond with a justification, something like, 'It was impossible not to get angry in that situation.'

These seemingly objective standards are based on the value system or notions that were formed in the environment in which we grew up, and the experiences we have accumulated. The standards we use to judge whether a situation justifiably warrants our anger are completely subjective. We believe that our standards are objective, and thus fair, but they're actually the products of our own thoughts, preferences and experiences. When we become angry, it is not really because of what someone else has said or done; it is because we consider ourselves to be right and others to be wrong. Our habit of judging everything as right or wrong ignites the fuse inside us. Rather than the situation itself, what makes us angry is our thought that something did not meet the standards that we consider to be 'correct', 'reasonable', or 'objective'. We judge people and situations according to our own standards, and we get angry when they fail to meet them.

There is no absolute yardstick with which to measure something as either right or wrong. Fundamentally, there is no right, and there is no wrong. Considering yourself as the standard causes others to be wrong. If you claim your standards are objective, you are proclaiming yourself to be absolutely right, and people will likely think of you as stubborn, self-righteous or rigid.

Those who have a strong sense of right or wrong are easliy angered. Those who are less rigid about what is right and what is wrong are less likely to get angry. When you let go of your subjective yardstick, there is no reason for you to insist that you are right or to judge others as wrong and criticize them. Then, you are not so likely to get angry.

This doesn't imply that you should think that others are always right. It's not possible to say that your child who is addicted to gaming or your partner who drinks excessively are 'right'. You can, however, come to understand that the reason your child and partner behave in this way is because of their own longstanding habits. It's important to accept others as they are, rather than judging them based on your own thoughts and standards.

You might come home to find your child totally absorbed in playing computer games, not even acknowledging you as you walk in the door. You become very angry and shout. After acting out in anger, you are sorry and feel bad.

The next day, you come home from work to find your child playing computer games yet again. How will you react this time? Because you felt sorry about shouting the day before, you try to suppress your anger and talk calmly. Your hesitation to yell or lecture isn't the result of thinking about what is best for your child. You hesitate because you're not sure which course of action is better for you – saying nothing and feeling frustrated or becoming angry and launching into an inevitable conflict.

The child, however, is doing nothing more than playing computer games and having a good time relaxing at the end of the day. Because you view the child's actions based solely on your own thoughts and standards, you judge this behaviour to be a waste of time and you become angry.

People generally think of suppressing anger as a positive thing, but venting anger and suppressing anger are more or less the same. In both cases, you are judging other people's actions based on your own standards, and you are still feeling the anger. The only difference is whether or not and how you choose to express your emotion.

If you become angry because your child does not meet your expectations, the standards you have set, and you scold them, you are simply taking your anger out on the child. The child won't want to listen. You want to say something but decide to back off just this once.

Swallowing your anger is also not desirable because it will raise your stress levels. In any case, suppressing your anger will not solve the problem. There is only so much suppression you can put up with before the emotion you are trying to ignore will need to find an outlet.

A man once asked me if getting angry at people who break social rules was justified. He told me, 'I get angry at people who don't obey traffic signals when I'm driving. I want to chase after the cars that cut in front of me without signalling and get even with the drivers. Surely those who do break these kinds of rules should be punished, shouldn't they? Otherwise how can the world function properly?' Some people seem to think that anger about a violation of such rules is somehow more justified than anger about personal or family matters.

But there is first something we must consider. Did the driver who cut in front of this man's car create the anger that he experienced, or did the anger rise from inside the man himself? Let me give you a simpler example. If you feel sad looking at the moon rising over a hill, did the moon make you sad, or did looking at the moon make you sad? Some people feel joy when looking at the moon. Some people feel other emotions, such as awe. Therefore, we can see that it is not the moon that makes people happy or sad. The emotion experienced emerges from within the minds of the people looking at the moon.

Let us apply this same principle to the man's road rage problem. If he becomes angry after a car cuts him off when he is behind the wheel, did this anger arise from within the man himself, or did the driver in the other car make him angry? All we did was replace the moon with the other driver, yet people feel confused by this concept.

The situation is clearer if we consider whether or not everyone in the same situation would behave the same way. The truth is that some people get angry when someone cuts them off while driving, some don't. Some drivers might just make room for the other driver and carry on. Some might curse under their breath but just keep driving. But others will express their anger by driving dangerously in retaliation or even go so far as resorting to violence.

In the end, we can see that there is no one situation guaranteed to arouse anger in everyone. The cause of our anger lies within ourselves, so whether we become angry or not depends on how we respond to the situations we face.

In this world we share, many different things may happen, and many kinds of people exist. We can't meet or avoid only those whom we want to meet or avoid. Even those we love may not always behave the way we think they should. To be free from suffering, we have to be constantly aware of how we discriminate between right or wrong, based on our karmic consciousness. We should practice letting go of our own standards, instead of imposing our standards on others. Then, no matter what situation we find ourselves in, or what kind of person we meet, we can avoid any unfortunate incidents caused by our inability to control our own anger.

Neither Suppressing nor Venting Anger: A Third Path

When we become angry, we usually do one of two things: vent it or suppress it. We think of these as the only possible responses to anger, but there is in fact a third way.

Recently, a woman asked me how to deal with her anger: 'When I'm angry, I don't talk about it, instead I tend to suppress it. The cause of my anger often seems too trivial to talk about, but it makes me angry not to say anything. Would it be better to just spit it out, or would I be better off continuing to suppress my anger, as I do now?'

If you vent your anger, the person you are angry with will probably also get angry, and thus the anger expands. This makes venting the worst possible option. However, if you swallow your anger, the anger will not expand outward to others, but you are likely to get stressed and perhaps even become ill, so this is not a good choice either. If you keep swallowing your anger, you might even suffer from symptoms such as a stiff neck, headache or blurred vision.

Many women of my mother's generation suffered from the symptoms of repressed anger. Sometimes a psychiatrist would incite the patient to vent her anger as an emergency treatment. By encouraging the patient to express her anger appropriately, rather than continue holding it inside, the symptoms would be somewhat alleviated.

However, this is just an emergency measure, rather than a fundamental solution to the problem of anger. Like adding a bit of cold water to a boiling pot, it helps to momentarily suppress the energy, but the anger will inevitably boil over again.

Some believe that those who swallow their anger are better people because they don't express negative emotions or upset others, but repressing anger does not make anyone happy. When you swallow your anger, you're more likely to experience stress and suffering, which is far from happiness (a state free of suffering).

A Brahman once cursed the Buddha, accusing him of stealing one of his followers. When the Buddha didn't reply, the Brahman bragged that he had won an argument against the Buddha. Of this, the Buddha said, 'Foolish people say they have won after cursing and slandering others. However, the real victory belongs to the one who knows the right way to respond. You should know that it is foolish to respond to an angry person with your own anger, because that means you have been dragged into their emotions and you have lost to them. It also means that you could not control your own emotions, so you also lost to yourself. It is a double defeat.'

The Buddha had listened to the Brahman without saying a word, not because he believed the Brahman was right, but because the Buddha understood that the Brahman's background and circumstances made it possible for him to say the things he said. The Buddha not only understood the Brahman's circumstances but also felt compassion toward him. Other people might wonder how the Buddha could endure such an insult, but the Buddha did not have to endure anything. He simply stayed calm because he fully understood and acknowledged the Brahman's situation.

When you reflect on the fundamental reason behind your anger, you are able to reach a state of being where anger doesn't arise. When you think

'I am angry because of you,' you need to think carefully about whether this is really true. Ask yourself the following:

> Why do I get angry when my child acts that way?
> Why do I suffer when my partner acts that way?
> Why do I get stressed when my boss acts that way?

You must be able to question the root of your own emotions. If you think critically before being swept away by these emotions, you may conclude that you have nothing to be angry about in the first place. You get angry, not because of your child, partner, or boss, but because of yourself. You feel frustrated, miserable, or sad because you stubbornly insist on the correctness of your own opinions, preferences and thoughts.

However, after deeper introspection, you may discover that there is absolutely no reason or justification for your anger. As a result, you will eventually be able to reach a state where you don't get angry about anything.

We think of our emotions as true and inherent, but they are actually formed through our habits. When we are constantly enslaved by our habits, they determine our fates. You get angry in the present because the seeds you have sown in the past have finally sprouted. If you continue to get angry, you will sow still more seeds that will bear negative fruit in the future.

Of course, it is not easy to see that there is never any reason to get angry, so we keep failing. But by continually trying to maintain awareness that anger arises from inside yourself, rather than attempting to repress feelings of anger, you will find yourself able to avoid anger more often.

If your habit is to become angry ten times a day, getting angry nine times a day is an improvement. If your habit has been to cling to your anger for more than an hour, you may find that your anger dissipates in under ten minutes once you acknowledge that you have become angry again. This is also an improvement.

It is easy to understand why we might call an angry person 'mad' when we observe their behaviour. If someone were to threaten you with a knife, the most reasonable response would normally be for you to run away, but if you become very angry, you may instead lift up your shirt, thrust out your stomach, and shout something like 'I dare you!' Obviously, at that point, you are not in your right state of mind.

Even though you may habitually get angry, if you remain aware of yourself and acknowledge that you are once again growing angry because you believe that you are right and someone else is wrong, you won't be carried away by your emotions. Just as the spark generated by a flint dies out in the absence of tinder, without that deep-held belief that you are right, your anger will dissipate.

If you continue to practice this self-awareness, eventually you will become angry less often. Even if you fail to notice that you are getting angry at the exact moment the emotion arises, you can subsequently recognize that you failed to catch yourself and so it becomes more likely that you will catch yourself at an earlier stage next time. Instead of blaming some other person for your emotional state, you will find yourself gradually changing. You may get angry less frequently, and when you do become angry, the duration of your anger should become progressively shorter.

When someone is angry with you, one way to avoid getting angry yourself is by responding with silence rather than immediately displaying your emotions in return. Once you've had a chance to gather yourself, try taking this a step further and smile if someone is behaving negatively towards you.

At first, you'll fail 90 per cent of the time. You may manage to smile with your lips, but you won't be able to smile in your heart. Even so, force yourself to smile and try it again tomorrow, and the day after tomorrow. If you practice not being swept away by other people's emotions, you may eventually find yourself free from other people's actions.

When Feeling Indignant About Not Having Retorted to What Someone Said

If someone criticizes you unfairly or wrongly accuses you, but you are not able to say anything at the time, you may think to yourself later, 'I should have said something.'

In the moment, you couldn't think of anything to say. But later, things that you feel you should have said come to mind. A woman asked me for advice, saying that she felt resentful and furious about not having responded to someone: 'Some time ago, I quarrelled with a coworker who lashed out at me in anger. But in the moment I couldn't think of anything to say – my mind went blank. Since then, I've felt increasingly regretful as I keep thinking of the things I should have said. How can I respond appropriately in those situations instead of behaving like a fool?'

If you want to think of something appropriate to say when faced with a situation, you need to remain emotionally detached from the situation. You can't say something appropriate when you're embroiled in confrontation because you are too angry, resentful, distressed or anxious to see things clearly. Once the situation has passed and you have calmed down, you may be able to think of all the things you should have said.

When someone swears at you, you are likely to get angry and swear back. Standing your ground may make you feel good in the moment, but you're likely to regret it later. If, on the other hand, you just repress your anger, you may feel you behaved like a fool or a coward. If you are not seized by anger, you won't get entangled in another person's emotions. If you can gain enough understanding of the angry person and consider how awful they must be feeling to say such things, you might be less likely to become angry in response. You may even be able to say something comforting. Detach yourself from the situation. Getting angry in response to another person's anger means that you are being dragged down into their negative emotions.

Another important method is to let go of your desire to 'get even'. You search for things to say because you want to defeat someone whom you see as an opponent in this situation, which you are regarding as a competition. Later you feel resentful and angry because you couldn't think of anything to say that would win the verbal battle. I think the real question this woman wanted to ask me was something more like, 'How can I defeat the other person verbally?'

In such a situation, the best way to become free is to rid yourself of the desire to defeat the person with whom you find yourself in contention. If you do find a way to win the verbal battle, you are likely to have accomplished this by hurting your 'opponent's' feelings. If you hurt your own feelings, you can always correct this when you realize that you've managed to hurt yourself. When you hurt someone else, there is no way to take back the injury, even if you later repent your actions and even if you apologize.

As an example, if your partner breaks up with you, you are likely to get angry. You may even feel that you should have left the relationship first. If you are the one to instigate a break-up with someone, and later realize that you made a mistake, it would be difficult to rectify the situation. But if they break up with you, you may feel distressed, and your pride might be hurt. In this case, however, you just need to heal your own hurt feelings, rather than also dealing with the guilt of having hurt someone else.

Wise people know it is better to be hurt themselves rather than to hurt someone else because ultimately the former entails less suffering than the latter. Hating someone will not only distress you but will also rob you of the freedom to see that person because you will most likely try to avoid them. Hate acts like a mental restraining order. If we don't hate anyone, we can go anywhere freely and see anybody with ease.

Yet we keep imprisoning ourselves. To live freely, you must let go of your desire to defeat, or get even with others, even if you believe that letting go of this desire will make you feel like a fool. It's better to look like a fool than to keep going with your hate. The truly foolish are those people who act smart when they're not. Acting smart, thinking you are better than others, is a continual effort. Putting an end to a potentially confrontational situation by simply saying that you were wrong is much easier, since you don't have to rack your brain for just the right words to defeat the other person.

Losing an argument should never be considered a defeat.

After all, only those who have a desire to win can be defeated. If you have no desire to win, you will never be defeated.

Transforming Existing Wounds into Life Assets

Although it might seem surprising, we often get hurt by a family member or someone close to us. In most cases, however, we suffer because we remember something as having been hurtful, when it actually wasn't. Even hurtful things that happened a long time ago will continue to cause us to suffer because we can't let them go.

For instance, most people who say that their parents hurt them forget the many beneficial things that their parents did for them. They resent their parents in the present based only on their memories. They may say, 'My parents sent my brother to an expensive college but they didn't do the same for me,' or, 'Whenever my siblings and I got into a fight, my parents only scolded me.' Once we have heard a good number of these stories, something interesting becomes clear; it seems that not many people actually recall having hurt others themselves, but so many feel that they have been hurt.

I met a woman who was deeply hurt because her mother had left home, abandoning her. She cried telling me how, decades later, she met her mother but still couldn't let go of feeling hurt and upset. 'My mother is over seventy now but I just can't forgive her. Sometimes I feel so tormented that I wonder if I should make peace with her, but I don't feel that I know how to do that after so much time has passed.'

The woman's tears were not in fact a result of the hurt of being abandoned by her mother, but from clinging to the hurt she felt when she was abandoned in the past. It was the memory of being abandoned that was making her sad, not the abandonment itself.

Most of our suffering is caused by our memories rather than actual events. We dwell on our misery by conjuring up memories of the times when we were disappointed or bullied, or in some other way damaged by others. Yet we are the ones who expand and reproduce our pain, by preserving clear images of things that happened, and then clinging to those images. It is almost like we choose to lock ourselves in a dark cave, within only these memories for company.

Harbouring resentment towards others and bad memories of the past deep inside our minds and constantly brooding over them is like watching a movie. When we recall a past event, our brain mistakes the imagery we create for an event happening right now, in the present, in front of our eyes. When we recall something good, we involuntarily smile, and when we recall something painful and sad, we may cry or feel heavy-hearted.

Our emotions arise unconsciously. If we preserve the emotional pain we experienced in the past, our current lives are likely to be miserable. These memories exist only in our minds; they have no tangible reality in the present moment. When we habitually recall the past, it's like we are repeatedly watching the same video clip over and over again. Many of us know people who only like to talk about 'the good old days,' as if they are still living in the past.

All our emotional wounds exist only in our minds, which hold onto these events and ideas as memories. We suffer, not because someone hurt us, but because we feel hurt over past events that may or may not have caused injury at the time. We harbour that hurt in our minds, and then continue to dwell on our hurt feelings.

Do not carry the past on your shoulders like a crushing burden. If you clearly understand that your present unhappiness originates from your own memories, healing your emotional wounds becomes simple. You can choose to break away from the past. Instead of dwelling on your sadness by continually replaying memories in your head, you can redirect your attention to the here and now.

It may be true that your mother abandoned you, but she might have been in a situation that forced her to do so, a situation of which you were never aware. When you're little, you are easily hurt, so you might have been bewildered and resented your mother at the time. But now that you've grown up enough to become a parent yourself, you should try to understand that she may have had no choice but to abandon her own child. The choice may have been a very difficult one for her to make. At that point, you might find yourself able to feel differently. You might even think: 'Mum, thank you for giving birth to me. I am in this world thanks to you.'

If you were to stop resenting your mother and start thanking her instead, you might gradually stop feeling gloomy and begin to brighten up. This might help you stop feeling like a victim who was abandoned and unloved.

Other than yourself, there's no one in the world who torments, hurts, or makes you feel anxious. You suffer because you harbour negative memories deep inside. Understanding this will begin your healing process.

Everyone in this world can be happy. No matter how awful your experience was as a child, it's now in the past. If you stop replaying the stored film clips in your head, you can choose to be happy at any moment. The present moment is the only moment in which you actually exist. If you concentrate on the present, you will be free from suffering. Furthermore, if you can concentrate on the present, difficulties you experienced in the past may be turned into valuable assets. Perhaps your business failed, you broke up with your partner, or were hurt by someone. If you accept all these life events as precious experiences that help you to learn and to understand your life, they will enable you to deal wisely with whatever comes your way.

Regret Results From Clinging onto Past Mistakes

'If only I hadn't made that mistake. If only I had done something else instead.'

When people say such things, regretting their past actions, it may come across as self-reflection or introspection, but such words convey the message that the speaker is, at that moment, not happy. Feelings of regret may involve the act of repenting past wrongdoing. But for the most part, regret is about tormenting ourselves by not being willing or able to forgive ourselves for mistakes we've made in the past. When we experience regret, we need to carefully observe our state of mind.

A woman once told me that she regrets saying hurtful things to her mother: 'My mother lives in the countryside all by herself. She often complains that her children don't understand her, and that it's no use raising children. I understand how she feels and am sorry she is not happy, but when she blames us,

I become resentful. A few days ago, I lost my temper when she complained, and since then, I haven't called her. I really regret that.'

Many people experience conflict with their parents. Most children who don't understand their parents eventually come to understand them better as they themselves age. When children are young and rebellious, they don't listen, no matter what their parents try to tell them. When they grow up and have children of their own, they come to realize how many difficulties their parents must have experienced in raising them.

Only once you grow older and become less able, when you end up living alone after losing your spouse, will you then be able to understand the loneliness of an aged, isolated mother. Even though you may not really be able to understand how older people feel, if you try to understand them and ease their loneliness, perhaps you may not feel as lonely when you yourself grow old. You could take care of your own mother in order to prevent or lessen the suffering you yourself may experience when you grow old, in addition to doing it for your mother's sake. Parents who live a hard life in the countryside may assume that their children will take care of them, and they will be able to live comfortably after retirement, after a life of hard work and sacrifices to raise their children. The surprising reality is often that when the children grow up, they are so busy making their own living that they hardly visit their parents. Because parents feel lonely, they lament their fate. They grow disillusioned with their circumstances and disappointed with their children, and, out of resentment, may say things like, 'How could my children be so uncaring, when I sacrificed so much to raise them?'

It is not difficult to solve this problem if you can think about what your parents went through to raise you. You just need to shift your thinking, instead saying, 'I am sorry I don't visit you often enough.' If you repent in this way, you will stop feeling resentful even when your mother blames you. If your mother says she's disappointed in you, you can empathize with her and say, 'You're right. There is no benefit in raising children!' This will not only comfort your mother, but it will ease your own feelings as well.

If, however, you think to yourself, 'Oh not this again, there she goes saying the same thing over and over. It's not like she's the only person who ever raised children,' what your mother says will feel to you like moaning and complaining. You will come resent her and perhaps even feel irritated and frustrated. When you feel frustrated, you are more likely to argue, resulting in unpleasant interactions which will make you even more reluctant to call, which will, in turn, leave you feeling regretful and sad.

If your mother were to suddenly die immediately after you have a falling out, you would no doubt be regretful and blame yourself for having been a terrible child to her. If you don't want to repeat such foolish behaviour, you should care for your mother to the best of your ability. If your habit has been to call every week, try calling her twice a week. If you have visited twice a year, try to visit four times a year. If you presently visit every month, you should make the effort to visit her twice each month.

You should try to relieve her deep sorrow with twice the effort you were making before. Her sorrow is not just her own. When she passes away, it will become yours, and you will regretfully think, 'I should have been kinder and more patient when she was alive.' If you have such regret in your heart, you will feel a deep sorrow. Being kind to your parents now will benefit you in the end.

It's foolish to regret and to blame yourself for past wrongdoings. To regret is to hate yourself for making a mistake, or for failing to deal with something properly. Regret is, in fact, a form of self-abuse. Your inability to forgive yourself for making mistakes usually stems from subconsciously thinking too highly of yourself, which makes you unable to accept that you, like everybody else, can make mistakes. Usually, you regret your behaviour because you think of yourself as an exceptional person.

Not being able to forgive others is hate; not being able to forgive yourself is regret. Regret is different from repentance. You regret because you cling to the idea that you are an extraordinary human being. Regret occurs when you berate yourself with the idea that such an outstanding person as yourself should not have acted so foolishly or fallen into making such a mistake. If you can acknowledge and accept that you are not in fact so outstanding and extraordinary that you will never make mistakes, you will no longer feel regret.

If you regret something, you will dwell on it. Repentance happens when you realize that you made a mistake, resolve never to make the same foolish mistake again, and move on. If you fall down, crying serves no constructive purpose. You should just get up and try to make sure that you don't stumble in the same way again. The first step in repentance is contrition about past wrongdoing, and the second is making every effort never to do it again.

Humans are not particularly special. We make mistakes and do wrong. Instead of blaming yourself, tell yourself, 'I have done wrong. I will not make the same mistake again,' and then move on. Rather than regretting and blaming yourself, repent and move forward.

Anxiety Is the Result of an Obsession with the Future

In addition to making ourselves miserable by clinging to past events we cannot change, we also worry and feel anxious about a future that has yet to arrive. Even though the future has not happened, many people incessantly worry about it and even fear it.

'What if I fail the exam?'

'What if I get sick?'

'How should I spend my old age after raising my children?'

We cannot seem to let go of our worries, even for a moment. As if it is not enough to be tormented about a past that has already disappeared, we are anxious and worried about things that have not yet, and may never, happen. We are anxious about things we are imagining.

A single woman in her mid-thirties told me about her anxiety about the future: 'Since I work freelance, I'm occasionally seized with anxiety and worry about my old age. Rather than my lack of a stable income, it's my lack of a clear plan or goal that causes these fears. When I was young, I always had goals I wanted to achieve and worked hard toward them. But at one point, it occurred to me that I didn't need to work so hard, so I quit my job. Right now, my mind is at ease, but I sometimes feel anxious and confused about whether it is the right choice to live day to day without a goal.'

It seems contradictory that she feels confused when her mind is at ease. If she wants to live a frantic lifestyle because of her job, she can do so. But having stopped living such a hectic life because she thought it was a problem, surely she should now lead a relaxed life. The reason the young woman felt anxious and questioned whether it's all right to live without a goal is that, until that point, she had been working so hard toward her goals that her habit of frantic goal-seeking had not yet been broken. Her habit remained in her subconscious, and now that she wasn't working so hard, she felt anxious about lagging behind others and wasting time. She was like a smoker trying to find better quality cigarettes, rather than simply quitting the habit of smoking. Or maybe like an alcoholic trying to get better liquor rather than trying to stop drinking.

Smoking is always worse than not smoking at all, no matter how high the quality of the cigarette. The same applies to drinking. You'll have nothing to worry about if you just let go of these habits and decide not to have them in your life. If you don't come to this realization, you'll falter and question your path whenever you run across what seems to be the best quality cigarettes or liquor.

When you see your friends drinking and smoking, you may ask yourself why you should be the only one excluded from the fun. This feeling indicates that you still haven't been able to completely break away from your drinking and smoking habits. Even the highest quality liquor and cigarettes have no value to a person who doesn't drink or smoke. Similarly, if you understand that money or status are not the way to happiness, there will be no reason for you to feel anxious watching other people earning a fortune or being promoted to lofty heights while you are making other choices and directing your energy elsewhere.

We can find examples in the natural world. Is there any purpose or goal to the Earth moving around the sun? No, the Earth simply rotates in accordance with natural laws. On Earth, plants germinate, grow, blossom and die. Is there some purpose or plan behind this? What purpose do squirrels and rabbits have in mind as they dash about so busily? What purpose do dolphins have as they splash amongst the waves? They are all simply leading their lives as they were born to do.

Humans are born, live as part of nature, and die, the same as a clump of grass or a rabbit. Living without thought about the purpose of life neither diminishes human dignity nor destroys the order of nature. There is no reason to be anxious about not having a purpose in life.

Our lives become miserable when we assume that life has a purpose. We grow anxious, restless and miserable because we give too much meaning to life. If you had breakfast this morning, what is there to be anxious about? If you have a warm place to sleep tonight, what is there to be anxious about?

The woman who came to me for advice chose to be a freelancer because she didn't want to be tied to a company, didn't want to work for somebody else, and didn't want to be bossed around. She wanted to live as she pleased, sleep when she wanted, travel when she wanted, and write when she wanted to write. In fact, it is not at all true that she had nothing she wanted to do; the fact is that she had too many things she wanted to do. Whatever she did, she wanted to do everything her own way.

She quit working for a company because she wanted to live as she wished. But then, she became anxious and restless because she was worried about what would happen in the future if she continued to live this way. Her attachment to the future made her anxious in the present.

Perhaps 80 per cent or 90 per cent of anxiety comes from thoughts about the future. To ease this restlessness and anxiety, we need to consider that today's troubles are enough for today. When I say this, people ask me how they can live thinking only about today. They assert that we must all think about tomorrow, the day after tomorrow, a year from now, ten years from now, and so on.

It is good to be prepared for the future, but if you think about it too much, you will have the same subjective experience as when you actually encounter that for which you are preparing – your mind becomes anxious and restless. This then becomes an illness of the mind.

Anxiety can affect one's physical health. A woman in her forties once told me that she felt something was wrong with her health, and that she couldn't sleep because she felt so anxious about it. 'I felt a lump in my throat and had some tests,' she told me. 'I'm waiting for the results, and it's hard not to be anxious and restless. How can I control my mind?'

When you find that something is wrong with your body, your options are simple: you can go to a medical professional and have your body examined. If you already had a test, you just need to wait for the results. If the lump in the woman's throat turns out to be simply an inflammatory response to stress or infection, or a benign tumour, her reaction should be gratitude for the good news. Considering that it might have been a malignant tumour, she should feel extremely grateful.

Even if it did turn out to be a cancerous growth, isn't it fortunate that this too can be treated? If she had found out a year later, it may have been more difficult to treat. The doctor's job is to treat the cancer, so the woman can entrust her treatment to her doctor. She might worry about the possibility of dying during surgery, but that's not something she can know ahead of time. Worrying won't make the surgery more likely to succeed, and not worrying won't make it more likely to fail.

In a situation like this, you have two options: the first is to pray that everything will turn out fine. You may think, 'I'm grateful that I'm able to have surgery. It's fortunate that this is operable.' The second is to take the opportunity to practice letting go of your attachment to the body. You can think to yourself, 'I thought I would live forever, but my body could collapse overnight! The body is not something to be attached to.'

With these realizations, you can live the rest of your life with a lighter heart. Whether it stems from a forthcoming test, a plan you are making, or a health problem, anxiety arises from a fixation on the future. Instead of worrying about the future, pay attention to what is happening in the present. Tell yourself repeatedly that everything will be fine, whatever the result may be, and you will gradually see your anxiety disappear.

Most of the time, we are not aware of the present moment. When we spend our days thinking about the past, or worrying about the future, we fail to be fully awake to the present. Happiness will not materialize on its own. When you focus on the present and do your best, these moments accumulate, and they can then continue to become your happy future.

Superiority Complexes and Inferiority Complexes Come From the Same Place

We usually compare ourselves to others and make judgements about ourselves. If we judge that our circumstances are better than those of others, we feel superior. If our circumstances are worse, we feel inferior. There is no absolute standard against which to measure your position. Our judgement depends on who we compare ourselves to.

A man I knew felt insecure about his looks because he was teased when he was young. He told me: 'My face is bigger than other peoples' faces. I've been teased a lot over the years because of it, which hurt and made me very insecure. As a result, I've been miserable and lonely for 37 years. I'm very sensitive and timid, so I have few friends. I don't even sleep well because I'm so dissatisfied. What should I do?'

I started by asking him a question in return, and it resulted in the following dialogue:

'Is this bottle big or small?'

'It seems small.'

'When you compare it with a table, is it big or small?'

'It's small.'

'When you compare it with a watch, is it big or small?'

'It's big.'

'Then, when you just look at this bottle by itself, is it big or small?'

'Isn't it about average?'

We make judgements about objects by comparing them with other things. We perceive an object as small in one context, and in another it seems large. When we say something is large or small, new or old, superior or inferior, old or young, long or short, we may believe we are making objective evaluations. But these evaluations are highly subjective and are based on nothing more than our own perceptions.

How you evaluate the size of someone's face will differ according to the size of the faces you compare it to. In any case, the size of the man's face was not the real problem. He just hadn't been able to heal the deep wound that was caused by the memory of other children mocking him and criticizing him.

When we look at ants in a colony, they appear to be identical. But if you were to take each ant and weigh it individually, their weights would differ. The relative sizes of their heads, antennae, eyes and abdomens would all differ as well. So, which ant is the good-looking ant, and which one is ugly? If you used a microscope to examine the ants, you might find that their faces were all different, but I don't think any one of them suffers from an inferiority complex about its looks. A fact or circumstance becomes a problem only when you believe it to be a problem. Differences in appearance are just differences. They're not problems in and of themselves. People with superiority or inferiority complexes will similarly accept the standards of others in different aspects of their lives. Feeling superior or inferior is a psychological phenomenon that occurs when people compare their lives with the lives of others as a tool to measure what they consider their own 'value' to be, instead of becoming the masters of their own lives. The feelings of superiority and inferiority have the same root.

An inferiority complex comes from delusions about, or high expectations of, oneself.

'I look okay, but my eyes are too small.'

'My face is mostly fine I guess, but my nose is so ugly.'

'My lips are all right, but my teeth look super weird.'

Oddly enough, celebrities (who we often regard as better looking or more talented than most people) are much more likely to be insecure about their appearances than ordinary people. After all, an inferiority complex is not caused by being unable to meet some absolute standard, but by being unable to meet one's own expectations. In order to push themselves to achieve in the way they do, most of these people have to set their expectations of themselves extremely high. This can only lead to anxiety about meeting these expectations, and disappointment or anger when they do not.

There are no inferior or superior beings in this world. All beings are simply different. If we were to pick 20 ordinary people and rate everything about them – their height, weight, hair, size of eyes and nose, length of arms and fingers, running ability, long jump ability, cooking ability, and so forth – we could evaluate them simply based upon various rankings. If we rank each person using only one trait, each member of the group would seem very different from the others. But if we rated 1,000 characteristics of those 20 people, their total scores would be pretty similar because even though everyone is different, overall, people are similar.

During certain historical periods, situations, or circumstances, only a few factors were used to rank people. During the Joseon Dynasty in Korea, the civil service examination ranked only literary ability. Yet in the current modern society, people with singing or dancing abilities are highly admired. If you were born a hundred years ago, your ability to pitch a ball well would have been useless, but right now you could potentially earn a lot of money as a baseball player. Even the most coveted ability will change according to the period of time one is living in, and the values prevalent in that period.

To be free from an inferiority complex, you need to recognize that it is nothing but a delusion. Even a physical disability is not an inferiority, but rather an inconvenience. For instance, if you can view having only one arm as merely inconvenient, you can overcome that inconvenience by learning to compensate or getting an artificial limb.

The first step to overcoming a superiority or inferiority complex and becoming happy is to take a postivie view of the situation. You may base this on the knowledge that all beings are simply different. A Buddhist monk, for example, should think of himself as a person who lives without a partner. If I compared myself to married people, I might feel inferior (or perhaps superior). This may also mean that I can't be satisfied with my life as a monk. But on the other hand, if I had not become a monk, I wouldn't have been able to give Dharma talks as freely as I do now. There are so many things I can do because I live the way I do.

When you feel bad about yourself you may think, 'I'm neither this nor that. What am I?' Try to change your thoughts to: 'I am this, and I am also that.' When you view your circumstances through a positive lens, things will have better outcomes, and you will become more confident in your life.

Feelings Arise, Stay, Change and Disappear

The body is composed of a combination of physical elements, and it changes according to its current state of health. Older cells die off and new cells grow to replace them. We think our bodies remain the same, but they're constantly changing as they continue the cycle of birth and death. Such changes are called birth, ageing, sickness and death.

It's the same with the mind. When an emotion arises, we may feel like it will last, but it soon scatters and disappears. This process consists of arising, staying, changing and disappearing. We want other people to stay the same, but that's an impossible expectation. Even though you may promise 'to love until death do us part,' your feelings may very well change over time. That is one of the characteristics of the mind. Being unaware of such characteristics and wanting other people to stay the same leads to suffering.

Feelings rise and fall from moment to moment; they have no substance in either shape or form. Still, we become worried and anxious, clinging to feelings of happiness, sadness or loneliness as they show up. A woman came to me for advice, worried that the love her partner felt for her might change following their marriage: 'I don't think it's bad to fall out of love while you're dating,' she said, 'but as I began thinking more seriously about getting married, I became worried about him falling out of love with me after marriage. I believe that once you are married, you can't simply replace your spouse when your feelings towards them change; you have committed to staying married to that person for the rest of your life. Since I began thinking this way, my love life hasn't been going well. Maybe it's because my mind is burdened with this thought. Is there any way for feelings not to change or to change for the better?'

Of course, this is not possible. The mind cannot remain constant. One moment you like someone, the next moment you may feel differently. One moment you and your partner seem like a match made in heaven, and the next something happens that makes it feel like you are sworn enemies. The mind keeps changing. That is the nature of the mind, and it cannot be judged as right or wrong.

There is a saying, 'Once on shore, we pray no more,' which explains how a change in our circumstances tends to shift our feelings as well. We feel differently when we borrow money from a friend, compared to when the time comes to repay it. Also, we feel different about our partner when we are dating compared to when we are married. Once you're married, you may grow weary of the work involved in sustaining your relationship; you may become attracted to someone else and want to date them. Rather than denying such feelings, you need to simply refuse to act on them. If you knew negative consequences would result from acting on your desire, you wouldn't do so. Likewise, if you know that you will suffer a loss if you don't do something, you will likely find a way to go ahead and do it.

When you are dating someone, it's easier to break up if that's what you decide to do, because the relationship isn't legally binding. If your partner no longer loves you or you become tired of your partner, it is better to break up. You will suffer less by ending the relationship at that point. If, after getting married, you continue to follow your desires, the negative consequences will be worse.

For that reason, you need to practice moving beyond your momentary impulses rather than acting on them.

Of course marriage is no guarantee that your feelings will remain constant. In fact, it is impossible to have positive feelings toward your spouse all the time. When negative emotions arise, rather than being swayed by them, you have the option of taking a long-term perspective on your life: essentially, emotions arise and then disappear.

If you're aware of this, you can avoid any damage that could result from impulsive actions arising from your emotions taking control of you.

The path to happiness doesn't depend on feelings remaining constant, but on understanding that feelings inevitably change and that you are not obliged to follow your feelings with actions. Realizing this, you can have a peaceful life free of the extremes of high excitement or deep depression. No matter how strongly we demand that someone remains utterly steadfast in the way they feel, this is still an impossibility. All we can do is accept that people's feelings change. In the case of married life, you must choose whether or not to stay with your spouse despite a change in feelings.

Feelings arise, stay for a while, change and then disappear. The process may differ from person to person and one relationship to another, but the experience is common to everyone. We mistakenly believe that feelings won't change, so as a result, we suffer. If you know how the mind works, you can be free of the suffering that comes from vainly trying to change others (or stop them from changing) or from hating others for changing, or for not changing in the way you would like them to.

Formed Habits Can Be Changed

A pine tree may take root in a crevice between rocks on a cliff – for this to happen, and for the tree to survive, there must be constant interaction between the tree and its environment. Humans are the same. Our habits and behaviours take root over time through our interactions with our environment. Our personalities grow out of habits, and they don't change easily because they are a form of unconscious inertia. However, we often want to change our habits quickly, and this may cause us to fail. As a result, we tend to blame ourselves and think, 'I am the problem.' Likewise, we get annoyed and angry when others can't change their habits.

We often become impatient about our habits not changing as quickly as we would like them to. Having made the decision that we should change, we become frustrated with ourselves when that change is not instant. We respond by getting angry, hating others, or feeling discouraged. As habits are so deeply rooted in our subconscious and as a result are very difficult to change, some say that we are destined to be that way. However, all habits have been acquired, and because nothing is permanent, habits can be changed. This does, however, require a lot of effort.

If you want to quit smoking, a conflict will arise between your conscious desire to stop and your habitual, behavioural pattern developed at the subconscious level. The inertia of ingrained smoking habits conflicts with the new desire for change, and this may become a battle.

Our desires arise from our subconscious, whereas willpower is part of our conscious mind. When consciousness tries to control the subconscious, it fails most of the time. Some say, 'Resolutions do not last more than three days.' Trying to control the subconscious with conscious intentions rarely works. As a result, we are sometimes tempted to do things we know would be wrong either ethically or morally. We say that we know what we should and shouldn't do, but our actions do not always follow our intentions.

Words and actions are more influenced by the subconscious mind than by conscious thought or will. During exam time, students know that they should study but they may become tired and doze off because their instinct to relieve fatigue by falling asleep is stronger than their will to study. Consider a student who is preparing for an important test. She asks her mother to wake her at 5am. Then, just to be on the safe side, she also sets her alarm before she goes to sleep. When her mother wakes her and the alarm rings, she opens her eyes briefly, but then goes back to sleep. In the morning, she complains that her mother didn't wake her up. But if, instead of studying for her exam, she had been leaving to catch a flight for an exciting holiday, it is likely she would have woken up earlier without even needing an alarm or wake-up call.

This is the difference between conscious and subconscious behaviour. Deciding to wake up at a certain hour is an act of consciousness. But when you're asleep, you are in a subconscious state. Waking up earlier than usual because of a dream, or in anticipation of an exciting event, is an act of subconscious guidance. Most often, only the things that you feel strongly about, things that move you deeply, can influence the subconscious.

You might make a conscious decision that feels to you like a firm resolution, but it won't last unless it is accepted by your subconscious. Even though your conscious thoughts have changed, your behaviour won't change unless your subconscious changes too. The reason it is difficult to overcome your weakness – even when others keep reminding you about it and you make sincere efforts to change yourself – is that your will to overcome it isn't able to override the resistance posed by the inertia of your subconscious.

It's not easy to change unconscious behaviour, but neither is it impossible. If you have a strong will, you can even change karma although it might seem that this is impossible. Before expecting any change to occur, however, you need to know that karma does not change easily.

Start to work on changing your karma with the awareness that there will be many stages of trial and error, and that it will take a long time. To change the habits that determine our fate requires steady effort and a strong will. The problem is that most people don't make a steady and consistent effort, or they don't have a sufficiently strong will. They try for a little while and then, when they don't quickly see the results they had hoped for, they give up. Perhaps they wonder why they should bother to change, and they may believe that they should just get on with their lives without changing their behaviour after all.

You need to believe that you can change and sustain your efforts over time. If you persevere, new habits will form and come to reside in your subconscious. As your habits change, eventually so will your fate.

Part 03

Living with People Who Hold Different Opinions

When we meet people, a certain mentality is at work. As we meet them for the first time, we start out with the premise that they are different from us. So, we put up our guard and probe them to reveal themselves, asking questions to find out more. If we find something in common, in terms of perspective, people we know, experiences, place of birth, or name, we are satisfied and befriend them quickly. We become friends, lovers, acquaintances or colleagues. Once we become close with them, our assumption that 'we are different' changes to 'we are the same.' As a result, our relationship appears to have become stronger.

However, this is when conflicts begin. We had come to think they were the same as us, but we find that they are different. We discover that they have a different personality, different views of the world, different ideas about politics, and a different palate. The fact is they haven't changed, we have just got to know them better. We thought they were the same as us and were compatible with us based on the little we knew about them. Then, we get into conflict with them because we think they are doing something unexpected or something wrong.

All Conflicts Stem From Relationships

In the course of our lives, we meet with and part from a countless number of people. When we meet someone we like, there's no problem. There's also no problem when we part from someone we don't like. However, we may feel miserable when we have to part from someone who we are fond of or uncomfortable when we have to meet with someone we don't like.

The Buddha referred to suffering in life as the '84,000 afflictions,' referencing the fact that humans experience countless different types of suffering. These afflictions are also referred to as the '108 afflictions' or 'eight sufferings.' The eight sufferings include 'the suffering of having to part from those you love' and 'the suffering of having to meet with those you dislike.' Again, you suffer if the situation calls for you to separate from someone you love, and you also suffer if the situation calls for you to be with someone you dislike.

Tolerating a spouse you dislike because you can't easily get a divorce is suffering. Alternately, you might love your partner but suffer because of having to live with a mother-in-law you dislike. Even though you like your job and are paid well, working with a boss or coworker you dislike causes suffering. When you dislike something, whether it's a marriage or a job, you would be fine if you could just quit. But if, for whatever reason, you can't escape the situation, you will suffer.

It is natural to think that because suffering is usually caused by relationships, the problem will be solved if we sever the relationship. In doing so, we refuse to meet with those we don't like, divorce a spouse, or leave home if we don't get along with a family member. But rather than making us happy, these actions are likely to make us feel lonelier and even more miserable. Suffering arises when we begin a relationship, as well as when we end one. When the relationship we formed (hoping it would make us happy) causes suffering, the reason lies not in the relationship itself, but in having formed the relationship for the wrong reasons.

Many people ask me questions about how to form romantic relationships, how to get married, how to raise a child, how to take care of their parents, and how to deal with their work life. All these questions appear different on the surface, but when we examine them closely, they're all based on relationship issues. Each relationship appears to be slightly different, but the principle at work is similar. Conflicts arising from relationships all stem from the fact that everyone is different. We tend to become disappointed and distressed because things we would like to have in common are in fact different.

Let's take a look at people's appearances. Are they the same or different? People have some common features, but there are often many differences. We all have eyes, a nose and a mouth, but upon examination we can see that these features have different shapes and sizes. The same applies to people's thoughts. Everybody thinks differently, but the closer we are to someone, the more we want them to have the same thoughts, opinions and feelings as we do. We become disappointed with them for not being as similar to us as we would like, and we resent them for not doing what we want them to do.

When you pick up a handful of soybeans and examine them, their size, colour and shape are all slightly different. At first glance, they may look the same, but when you look at them closely, they're different. But what about when you compare them with red beans? In comparison to how markedly different soybeans are from red beans, the slight differences among the soybeans become insignificant. Individual soybeans may differ in size, shape and colour, but when we compare them to red beans, they're all easily identifiable as soybeans. When the soybeans are compared to one another, they are different, but they are all soybeans.

The things we encounter every day have dual characteristics; they have both similarities to and differences from other things. Even when they're different in some respects, they are the same in others. When they're the same in some respects, they are different in others. Likewise, beings are neither the same nor different. When we say things are different or the same, the difference or the similarity lies not in the things themselves but in our perception of them. Beyond our perception, beings are just beings.

When conflict arises in a relationship because of a difference of opinion, there are two ways to resolve it. The first is to accept each other's differences, saying, 'I think this way and you think that way.' This doesn't mean that I'm right, and you're wrong or that you're right, and I'm wrong. It's simply a case of accepting that we are all different. Accepting someone who is different from us is equal to respecting that person. To respect the other person is to accept that person as they are, instead of judging them to be either right or wrong.

The second way to resolve a conflict in a relationship is to understand the other person: 'From that person's point of view, they would probably think more along these lines...' 'Because of my child's position, he would be most likely to behave that way.' 'From my partner's position, they could take it that way.' 'From the viewpoint of the Japanese, it's possible to come to that conclusion.' 'From the viewpoint of the North Koreans, they could take such a position to mean...' and so on. To think this way is to understand others.

Accepting and understanding that the other person is different from you is the most fundamental mindset to have when establishing relationships. If you can remember these two perspectives as you are forming a relationship, you will be equipped to prevent the majority of potential conflicts.

Good or Bad?

Everyone wants to have good relationships with good people. But what kind of person is a good person? How can we distinguish between a good person and a bad person?

A college student once asked me: 'As I get older, I'm meeting a lot of different people. What do I need to do to form relationships with good people? How do I know if people are good?'

So, I asked her in return, 'Are you a good person?'

She replied, 'I believe that I am a good person, yes.'

'You will find that everybody considers themselves to be a good person, so it can be difficult to tell who is actually good. How, then, should we distinguish between a good person and a bad person?'

'Shouldn't we start by distinguishing the factors that make a person bad?'

'But what is bad? Let's say a woman has been a good Catholic for more than 30 years but then decides to convert to Protestantism or Buddhism. What would the members of her Catholic church think?'

'I guess they would think she is bad.'

'What about Protestants or Buddhists?'

'I guess they would think she is great.'

'They would probably say she has finally come to her senses. In such a case, how is it possible to distinguish whether she is a good person or a bad person? Let's say you have a boyfriend, but you think he's not such a good person and break up with him. Will he remain single for the rest of his life, or will he meet other women?'

'I guess he'll meet other women.'

'Yes, after you break up with him, he will likely meet other women. If your boyfriend thinks you're not such a good person and breaks up with you, you will very likely meet other men. In this case, what is good and what is bad?'

'It depends on your viewpoint.'

'That's right. You said you wanted to meet a good person, so what do you think you should do?'

'Well, I guess I should choose a person who is good based on my perspective.'

'Do you think that your perspective will be the same as the perspective of your parents, or different?'

'It will probably be different. But I think I will like the person I have chosen because I perceive him to be good.'

The person you like will seem a good person to you. If someone else thinks that same person is bad, then that first person is bad from that person's perspective. Any person appears to be good or bad according to the karma of the one evaluating them. However, the fact is, no one is either absolutely good or absolutely bad.

When one perceives others to be either good or bad, each person is evaluating through a different framework of perception. Protestants and Buddhists have different frameworks of perception, just as if they were wearing glasses fitted with different coloured lenses.

Consider a man who worked hard and saved money for his old age. His wife, a devoted Buddhist, donates $100,000 to a temple without his knowledge. Those at the temple will think that the wife is a great person, but her family will most likely come to the conclusion that she is out of her mind. The same action can provoke opposite reactions in people, depending on their positions and views, and how the original action may impact them.

The standard we use when we describe someone as 'good' is really how well that person treats us. Those who are good to us can be divided into two categories: The first category consists of people who benefit us materially or emotionally. The second category consists of people who agree with us. Generally, people we don't like are those who do the opposite – they don't benefit us and they don't agree with us. All our efforts to distinguish between good people and bad people come from seeing the errors in our perception as objective realities. We say, 'They are a bad person,' when really we should say instead, 'Something about them bothers me.'

We mistakenly think of another person as being objectively bad when, in fact, it's simply a matter of us feeling that the other person is bad.

You will always encounter people you like and people that you don't like. If you form relationships only with those you like, you won't get to know so many people. If you insist on following your strict preferences, you will not be open enough or curious enough to learn the true value of interacting with different people. Instead, the range of people you meet and get to know will be more limited.

You need to meet many kinds of people in order to know and truly understand that people are different. If you want to meet good people, you must first open your heart to all people. If you can do this, you'll be able to meet and learn about all sorts of people. The result will be you learning to get along with a wide range of people.

No One Has Everything in This World

There are some people who have never been in romantic relationships, but the reason is not that there is anything wrong with them or that they are somehow lacking. When people with little dating experience talk to me about their love lives, they usually say something like: 'I'm at least average-looking, my personality isn't too bad, and my job is fine. So, why haven't I been able to have a romantic relationship? Why can't I get married?'

One possible reason might be that their standards are too high. If our standards are unreasonably high, approaching someone who meets those standards will be intimidating. It's easy to approach someone that we don't have such a high opinion of. It's much more difficult to approach someone who meets our highest standards. We believe there is better chance that they'll reject us, and their rejection will be more painful to us. This is similar to how we become tense when we're around someone in a high social position, or around someone who is rich or famous. We want to get acquainted with them, but we feel tense or fearful about whether they will accept us.

Another thing people often say is, 'There aren't many attractive people around,' or 'All the good ones are already taken.' If you find you are attracted only those who are already committed to other relationships, this may mean that you have unreasonably high standards or perhaps you are not truly ready for a relationship. Let's use work as an analogy. Many people want to work for a large successful firm or work as a lawyer or a doctor because those jobs are considered prestigious. Many competent and talented people covet such jobs, or only want to work in settings that offer particular work conditions. As a result, such jobs become difficult or impossible to find. In the same way, you may consider your standards to be quite reasonable when you are considering a prospective date, but on reflection it might become apparent that your standards are unrealistically high.

Perhaps your parents didn't get along well when you were young. When marital life is full of conflict or sadness, people may regret their marriages and say to their children, 'Your father/mother drives me crazy.' They complain about their spouses in front of their children, regardless of whether or not the children have the capacity to understand and process what's happening. Inevitably, the children develop negative feelings about one or both of their parents. Then, when the children grow up and enter into their own romantic relationships, they tend to have underlying feelings of anxiety. At a critical moment in a relationship, they tend to close down or run away. If you find marriage burdensome, this is very likely related to something you experienced as a child that remains in your subconscious.

The third reason might be a bad experience the person had as a child, such as emotional, physical or sexual abuse at the hands of an adult. Even though the incident might be forgotten (or at least not consciously remembered), such negative experiences could make them fear or reject marriage.

The last reason might be that they saw their friends or family members become miserable and resentful after break-ups. This might make them think to themselves, 'I should be very careful about whom I date – I don't want that to happen to me.'

Someone you initially thought was a good match for you might turn out to be otherwise after you have dated for a while. If you are not suited, it is not bad for the relationship to end in a break-up.

Looking at these possible reasons, you first need to uncover the reason why a romantic relationship does not seem to be happening for you. Once you discover the reason, you should be able to solve the problem and open your heart. When you look for a person with whom to have a romantic relationship, or when you get married, you become very selective. You can't date or marry just anyone, so you try to choose carefully. This is understandable, but if you have decided that you want a partner of a particular age, academic background, money, temperament and so on, it may be almost impossible to find someone who seems absolutely perfect. Thus, it may seem very difficult to get married.

In the old days, there were snake oil salesmen at rural markets who sold elixirs. They used to say, 'If you take this medicine, you will be cured of all illnesses.' They would hawk their medicines loudly and enthusiastically in the markets, and people would gather around, eager for healing. Obviously, there is no such panacea in the current world, but blinded and deafened by greed, people may be seduced by the idea of a cure-all. Relationships can work the same way. As is the case with possessions, no one person has everything. A sharp knife is useful for working in the kitchen, but it could cause bodily harm if a mistake is made or it is used in the wrong way. Cotton is soft, but it does not have a lot of strength. Everything in this world has such a duality.

Yet we are conditioned to want our prospective mates to possess every single desirable quality, including intelligence, gentleness, kindness, earning capacity, parenting skill, good looks and leadership. We want our spouses to be perfect and to excel in every possible way. Of course, this is impossible.

We develop certain expectations, and start comparing different people: 'Our next-door neighbour's husband does a lot of their housework. Why can't you help more?' 'Our next-door neighbour's wife just got another promotion. Why can't you work a bit harder?'

When we criticize our spouses in this way, it's just like choosing cotton for its softness and then complaining that we cannot use it to build a wall because it is not strong enough. Or like choosing a knife for its sharpness and then complaining that it is not as soft as cotton. There is no one perfect person in the world. It would be better for you to think, 'Well, no one has everything. The world is fair,' rather than getting annoyed at your spouse for not meeting all your expectations.

No matter how carefully you search in the forest, you just won't be able to find a tree that can be cut down and simply used as a pillar as it is. However strong and beautiful the tree may be, it must of course be trimmed, cut to size, seasoned, sanded and polished before being used. By the same token, if you're ready to adapt to others and find ways to compromise and get along with them, you will find you have many more relationship options. If you will only consider someone who will sweep you off your feet and make you feel like you are living in a romantic film, you will have a hard time finding someone to marry even if you search every corner of the world.

You only truly get to know someone after spending time with them and living with them. A woman may admire a man's decisiveness, but after living with him, she may find him to be stubborn, inconsiderate and set in his ways. Another may marry a man because he is sweet and easy to get along with, but after living with him, she may find him frustratingly indecisive. The qualities that seemed wonderful when dating might become unbearable as time passes and this may cause couples to break up.

If you're not good at dating, it's better to start by simply making friends or acquaintances. As the number of your acquaintances grows, so too does the chance that your circle may come to include someone for whom you develop special feelings. If you meet people simply as friends first and get to know them, without requiring that they tick all the boxes on your relationship-material checklist, it will be easier to find someone you might be compatible with.

If you go out to meet people with the goal of getting married, there will be very few people you can date after excluding those who are divorced, too old, too young or otherwise 'imperfect' according to the strict eligibility criteria you have decided on. Moreover, as a person you're interested in must also return your affections (and will likely have criteria of their own), it may turn out to be quite impossible to find someone to date at all.

Therefore, don't try to date only attractive people from the start. Tell yourself, 'Anyone will do. I will try dating casually with about five people, and then I may get into a serious relationship with the sixth.'

It's good to date people with such a relaxed mindset. It's better to break up while dating than divorcing them after getting married. It's better to get a divorce before you have children rather than later on when you do have children.

Breaking up is not necessarily a bad thing. If you meet someone and get married without ever having dated anyone else, you will miss many opportunities to meet other people. It may be better for everyone if they date several different people before committing to marriage with someone. However, if you date more than one person at a time, you may be criticized for being unfaithful or uncommitted. If your partner breaks up with you, it's not necessarily a bad thing. Then, you will be able to date other people without being criticized.

It is wonderful when you and your partner love each other and succeed in getting married, of course. However, you don't need to be hurt if someone leaves you, since this may give you the chance to find someone even more suitable. So do not be afraid that your boyfriend or girlfriend might leave you. If you decide to break up with them, this shouldn't be a problem either. These days, countless couples divorce, so breaking up with someone is no reflection on you.

After having dated three or more people, you will be able to understand people better. If you like your partner too much, they might feel burdened. If you are too standoffish, they might believe you don't care very much and they might leave you. The right approach is not achieved through planning – you can only arrive at it through multiple experiences. This is called the learning effect, and you can get the hang of it through trial and error.

As you practice how to deal with people by dating a variety of partners, you will learn to get along with people better and so experience fewer conflicts in your eventual marriage.

Conditions for a Happy Marriage

These days, it seems to cost a fortune and require months of preparation to get married. When choosing a prospective spouse, people carefully consider their partner's wealth and occupation. But are these conditions enough for a happy marriage?

A young man once asked me about what was necessary for a marriage to be happy and successful: 'I've always had a vague idea that if two people have the same values and goals, they will be able to have a happy marriage. But as I get older, people give me advice such as, "A man should have a certain amount in savings before marriage," or "You should be able to afford an apartment or a house in the city before you think about getting married." Everyone seems to think these things are so important, I just can't ignore them anymore. But what kind of values should I have in order to have a happy marriage?'

There are two major conditions for marriage. Firstly, in most countries, you must be over 18 years old. In other words, you have to be an adult. Secondly, you should be independent from your parents and be willing to share what you have with your spouse. Are you ready to adjust to sharing your home and your life with your spouse? You may want to go to the beach for your vacation, but your spouse would prefer to go to the mountains – what will you do? Are you able to accommodate their wishes instead of insisting always on just what you want?

For two people who have different personalities, thoughts, beliefs and ways of life to enjoy a happy marriage, each should be ready to give up half of their rights. Otherwise, no matter how grand their wedding, no matter how big their house, it will be difficult for the marriage to last. If you marry thinking, 'They'll accommodate my wishes as they did when we were dating,' without making any allowances of your own, you're guaranteed to run into conflicts.

Conflicts begin with trivial things. One partner puts away clothes neatly in the closet, but the other leaves them everywhere around the house. One thinks the food is too bland, but the other thinks the seasoning is perfect. One thinks the room is too hot and wants to open the window, but the other thinks it's too cold and wants the window to stay closed. One partner thinks it is important to shower every morning, while the other disagrees. Such differences between partners will lead to conflicts and fights. Trivial things like these make marriage difficult. In reality, the size of your apartment or the value of your car is not as important.

Many people considering marriage consider only these secondary things, without mentally preparing to adjust their lives to accommodate their spouses. Many marriages fail despite the abundant household appliances and other material goods that couples purchase thinking they will make their lives together easier. In some cases, these couples break up while in the middle of preparing for their wedding or decide to divorce soon after their honeymoon.

The system of marriage developed as it was thought beneficial to both parties involved. In general, the development of human civilization follows the path of maximum efficiency. If you and your partner each have a room but decide to live together, you'll save rent on one of the rooms and other costs. So, in that regard, marriage will benefit both of you. Living alone, you had to perform household chores by yourself, but when you get married, you can share the burden, which will allow you to have more free time. This allocation of roles directly benefits both partners.

But remember, living together for mutual benefit means that you need to consider the wishes of your spouse. Let's say the wife wants her husband to prioritize spending time together over making a lot of money. Then, instead of asking, 'Why do you complain so much when I earn a good living for you?' the husband should try to accommodate her wishes.

When you get married, you acquire the title of 'wife' or 'husband', along with some new responsibilities. Partners in a marriage need to accommodate each other's wishes. You don't need to strain yourself with the effort of fulfilling your role as husband or wife, but you should do the best you can to be a good partner.

When you're dating, physical attraction may be the most important factor. But if you want to have a long and happy marriage, you need to find someone willing to adjust to you and someone who will help you as you help them. For example, as marriage is communal living, you should be ready to do your share of cooking, cleaning and other household chores.

Of course, the most important condition for maintaining a happy marriage is willingness to get along with your spouse.

Are You Living a Truly Good Life or Just a Life That Looks Good to Others?

Many young adults find themselves having to make sacrifices due to increased financial pressures and unemployment. It seems natural that if someone manages to find solid employment, they would not only be happy, but would also be congratulated by others on this success.

A young woman once complained to me that she was miserable in a job she had started four months ealier but she felt she couldn't quit because her new position was at a prestigious firm: 'When I'm getting ready to go to work in the morning, I feel so distressed that I'm almost always on the verge of tears. I often cry at work, and by the time I come home, I'm heavy-hearted and feeling very sad and sorry for myself. I want to quit my job. However, people around me tell me to stick it out since it will be very difficult for me to get another job at such a prestigious firm, and because it's a great long-term job. But I feel so miserable every day, and I really don't know what to do.'

Let's imagine a smoker says to a non-smoking friend, 'This is an excellent cigarette. Try it.' The non-smoker tries it and finds that it hurts his throat and makes his eyes water. He doesn't like smoking anyway, but because his friend, the smoker, insists that the cigarette is first-class, he tries again. He continues to smoke through coughing fits and watery eyes. If smoking doesn't suit him, he can simply stop, but he's afraid to miss out on what he has been told is an excellent cigarette. So, he continues to smoke while complaining about the stinging throat. What a fool he is.

This is the same as hesitating to quit your job because others envy it and urge you not to quit. There is a saying that goes: 'No matter how highly-regarded the governor's position is, if you don't want it, that's that.' No matter how much others may commend and admire the job, if you hate it, it is not a good job for you. It may be a good job for somebody else. If you are miserable, you can simply quit.

Remember, it is your life, so why should you care what others think? Go to work, bid your farewell, and hand in your resignation.

If you can't bring yourself to quit your job, you need to think about the reasons for your hesitation. If the reason is money, you can always make money in other ways – there are many different kinds of jobs out there. Consider all the different jobs that people do.

Review a list of prospective jobs one by one. If you conclude that staying at your current job is the best option, that's great. If your position is stable and pays well, how can you expect to work without experiencing some difficulties? If you think, 'I don't want this job no matter how high the salary,' then there's really no need to carry on with it. You have thought long and hard about it, and concluded that you just don't want to do it.

The fact that the young woman shed tears while asking me this question means that she was conflicted – she felt the job was too good to quit but too stressful to keep. If you find yourself in this same situation, understand that the root cause of your suffering is conflicted desire, so you need to let it go. One option is to just hand in your resignation. However, if you can't afford to do so, try comparing your job with other types of work that are much more difficult. Tell yourself, 'I would only earn minimum wage doing manual labour, but my salary at my current job is twice that much,' and then go back to work in good spirits.

If you're struggling at work even though you managed to land a job that others are envious of, it may be that your abilities were overestimated. If your competency has been underestimated, you may feel a little disappointed. But that would be the end of it. If, however, your abilities are assessed too high to begin with, you may initially feel happy about receiving approval, but you'll soon feel a lot of stress. In order to meet those high expectations, you will have to work extremely hard and learn quickly in order to perform at the required level.

If your competency has been overrated at work, you may also feel added anxiety about letting others down. Inevitably, you will always be nervous and fearful that your incompetence might be exposed. In the worst-case scenario, this could lead to a loss of confidence or even mental exhaustion.

If your true ability level is 100 per cent it's best to represent yourself as having an ability of 80 per cent at most. This is the way to live your life with ease. If you were to have the ability level of 100 per cent but were thought to have the ability of only 50 per cent not many of your employers would criticize you, since they wouldn't expect very much. Over time, as they discovered that you were in fact performing significantly better than expected, they would be pleased with you, and you would gain recognition from those around you.

On the other hand, what happens if you were to have an ability level of 50 per cent but are believed to have the ability of 90 per cent or 100 per cent? When people begin working with you, they would find that your performance doesn't meet their original expectations, and they'd end up writing you off as incompetent. In such a case, your boss would become disappointed, and you would either end up being demoted to a lower position or turning in your resignation. Obviously, it is not wise to overstate your abilities.

To avoid being stressed by having your abilities evaluated at work, perform at your actual level of aptitude, instead of going to great lengths to do well or trying too hard to impress others. Accept the situation as it is. Doing the work is your job, but evaluating and reporting on your work is the job of management. There's an old Korean saying that goes: 'People do the work, and the heavens do the rest.' This means that you should do your best without obsessing too much about the results.

Even if you are able to think this way, it's not easy to change your long-standing habit of seeking praise. The greater the desire to perform well, the greater the disappointment when you are not given approval. Try to let go of the desire to do well, and just keep doing your work well with a light heart. Then, you will gradually see an improvement in your abilities.

The Boss Who Teaches You the Middle Way

Imagine how much people would enjoy their jobs if colleagues who spend a significant portion of their days together could be more understanding of each other and get along amicably. Most people say that interpersonal relationships at work are often more difficult than the actual work itself.

A woman I met who works as a nurse said she found it extremely difficult to satisfy her boss's demands: 'When my boss distributes work to the staff, she assigns five patients to me while assigning only four to the other nurses. When I sit down to work on the computer, she badgers me to get up and move quickly. When I move quickly to do as she demands, she changes her mind and says, "You're moving too fast and making others feel nervous. You need to calm down." I'm trying my best to adjust the way I work to her style, but I am finding it very difficult.'

When experiencing this conflict at work, the woman has two choices. She can choose not to work with someone like her boss and leave the job. However, if she can't quit, she needs to accept the situation as it is and find a way to make it work for her.

If we compare this situation to something like farming, imagine this – a farmer might think that the seed he's planting is good, but the field is in poor condition. In that case, the farmer would have to plough and fertilize the soil to enrich it, or plant the seed elsewhere in better soil. If the farmer can't afford to move to a new field, or if he has some other compelling reason for sticking with planting in the original field, his only option is to adjust to the current conditions of that field.

This won't be easy, but each of us must be willing to endure some hardships in order to make a living. Imagine you're going up a mountain to collect some firewood. You might complain that the mountain is too high to climb, that your axe is not sharp enough, or that the weather is too bad for cutting firewood, which would leave you no choice but to go back down the mountain empty-handed.

If the nurse wants to be happy where she is without leaving the hospital, she must change her perspective.

Her boss gave her more work compared to others, caring for five patients while others only cared for four, but she should actually see this as a good thing. She is competent enough to do this important work well. Since she is working anyway, it is likely better that she can take care of five patients, rather than not having quite enough to do while taking care of only four people.

If her boss asks, 'What are you doing?' when she's working on the computer, she should simply respond, 'I'm typing in data.' If her boss says, 'You're moving too fast and are making others feel nervous. You need to calm down,' she can respond by just slowing down a little. As she repeats this process, she will eventually find out the speed her boss prefers. This is important.

A nurse is paid for taking care of patients, and they accumulate blessings in the process. This is something to be thankful for. When her boss criticizes her for moving too fast, she should try to think, 'She is helping me learn the Middle Way.' The Middle Way is adjusting oneself to what another person thinks is appropriate. Doing this does not make you spineless or lazy. Rather, it's doing the best you can under given circumstances.

Again, the nurse's job is to take care of patients. People believe that nurses only need to care for patients, just as all teachers need only to teach their students diligently, but things are not so simple. Most organizations have managers, and it is important to get along with your boss if you want a pleasant working environment. You must be able to cater to your boss's disposition, as well as performing your job well.

This does not mean that you must flatter your boss or walk on eggshells around them. Just see your boss as one of the people toward whom you should be considerate. If your boss makes unreasonable demands, such as telling you not to take care of patients, to administer the wrong medication and so forth, you should of course refuse. Otherwise, as a coworker, you should learn to accommodate their wishes. If you can work amicably with such a demanding boss, they will find it easier to work with you, and are also unlikely to make things difficult for you if you eventually take another job elsewhere.

Think of your current job as a training opportunity to develop the ability to accommodate all types of people. If you find it impossible to work with your current boss, you can always quit and find a different job. If, however, you are treated unfairly according to the law, you should not simply quit. In such a case, you must exercise your legal rights as an employee to reach a fair solution.

Most Relationships Are Based on Selfishness

Most human beings are self-centred, and people usually want to form relationships that they feel will benefit them. When we seek to form and maintain a special relationship with someone, we have selfish motives, whether we're aware of them or not.

The same is true when choosing a prospective spouse. People select the person who will benefit them the most, taking into account various factors such as a person's finances, education, physique and personality. Even some aspects of parent-child relationships are based on selfishness, although of course in a different way. Children feel affection for their parents, not just because of their biological bond and because they have raised them, but because their parents are their principal benefactors.

As such, latent selfishness in human relationships may lead to conflicts over time. When dating someone, you may accept some small initial losses in the hope of bigger gains to follow in the future. This is like making a long-term investment.

Imagine you marry someone after dating for a while. Six months into the marriage, your feelings begin to change. You feel like you're not benefiting from the marriage as much as you had expected to, so you may end up feeling that you are actually running at a loss. Eventually, you may come to the conclusion that you would be better off living alone.

I'm not saying that being self-centred in your relationships is necessarily harmful, but you need to be aware that others are likewise motivated by selfish interests when forming relationships with you. If you can understand that others, like you, also calculate gains and losses in forming interpersonal relationships, you won't judge a self-centred person so harshly, and you will likely experience fewer interpersonal conflicts.

Imagine that your intention in some transaction was to give three items in the hope of receiving seven in return. Chances are, the other person may well have had the same intent for themselves. When each of you only receive three items, naturally you'll be disappointed in each other. Your dissatisfaction and disappointment are not caused by the other person but by your expectations of receiving a greater number of items for yourself.

A college student once consulted me on how to get along with an older student who she felt only treated her well when she needed something from her. The younger student considered this to be a detestable trait: 'There is a senior student who is the best student in our department. She's quite demanding and calculating. She is only nice to those she can control. For example, in class, several of us, including she and I, sit in the same row, but she only shares her food with people right next to her. I don't even like the snacks she brings, but it feels unpleasant to be left out. It annoys me that she seems to be nice to me only when she is trying to get something from me.'

If this student who consulted me marries someone and maintains the same perspective with which she perceives the senior student, she is almost guaranteed to have a failed marriage. If she views her partner from such a transactional perspective, she's likely to come to a point where she detests her husband. Imagine that she cooks for her husband, but he doesn't help her prepare meals, doesn't finish all the food on his plate, and says he is too busy to help when she asks him to do the dishes. She assumes he really is busy, but when she checks on him, she finds him taking a nap or watching the television. If her husband continues to behave this way, she will end up despising him and will not be able to stay in the marriage.

If she continues with the same mindset that she has toward the senior student, she is likely to view all the people around her in a negative light. For instance, when she gets a job, she's likely to end up despising her boss and coworkers, so she won't be able to remain in any job for long.

She is also likely to have problems dating. If she writes to her boyfriend twice, but he only responds once, or if she calls him three times, but he only calls her once, she'll get into an argument with him.

All humans have selfish tendencies. People generally make phone calls when they need something. I myself rarely ever call someone to ask, 'Do you need anything?' I usually call someone when I need help, and similarly most of the calls I receive are from people who have some kind of question of their own to ask me.

It's easy to think, 'Gosh, this person only calls me when they need something.' However, most people behave this way. Do politicians fawn over their constituents all the time? No. They do that only during election campaigns when they are keen to garner votes. So why are we better able to accept that politicans behave this way only when they need to?

It is up to the senior student to choose who she would like to share her snack with – whether it is the person right next to her or the younger student, or both of them. It is her right to decide, and her decision has nothing to do with anyone else. It would be better to think, 'It would be pleasant to be offered some, but if she doesn't, that's fine too.' You need to think this way.

It is only natural for the senior to ask the younger student questions about things she doesn't know. People often ask me questions when they are curious about something, and I also ask questions of others when I need information or am curious about something. Most people both give and receive help, it is the way of the world.

When you're always calculating potential gains and losses in your interactions with others, life becomes very tiresome. Parents give their children 100 per cent but the children don't give their parents even 10 per cent. Parents would be miserable if they expected their children to give them 100 per cent. The fact is that these parents probably also received 100 per cent from their own parents when they were children.

If we could somehow calculate the total amount of help that we give alongside the help that we receive throughout our lifetimes, the two would most likely be very similar. If we consider the whole, there may be some people like the senior student who seem to take more than they give, and there will of course be other people who will benefit you much more than you benefit them.

If someone offers you food, accept it and say, 'Thank you.' If they have food but don't offer to share with you, just think, 'That's fine.' They are doing whatever they want to do with what is theirs, so why should you get annoyed?

The same goes for dating. You may like someone, but it is not reasonable to despise them if they do not return your feelings. You have the freedom to like someone, and that person also has the freedom to like whomever they wish.

There's not even a need for you to resent your partner when they develop feelings for someone else.

Feelings change, and there isn't much you can do about it. If that happens, rather than being resentful, instead try to think, 'Well, I have been happy for the past two years thanks to you. I appreciate that time.' Then, even though the situation is difficult, you don't have to suffer from feelings of betrayal.

The human psyche combines both altruism and selfishness. During a crisis, people sometimes exhibit altruism, but they cannot be altruistic all the time. This is because altruism resides deeper in the subconscious than selfishness does. Thus, selfishness tends to emerge more easily and more frequently.

Once you acknowledge the fact that all humans have a selfish side, you can then focus on deciding to what extent you are willing to accommodate the demands of a selfish person. It is entirely up to you.

We don't need to rid ourselves of selfishness to achieve peace in the world. Simply understanding that others can be selfish, just as we ourselves can be, will drastically reduce potential conflicts.

Don't condemn or try to change other people. How do you expect that we can truly change others when we can't even change ourselves? It is, however, all right to encourage others to change themselves if this is for their own good, rather than because we currently disapprove of them or because them changing will make things easier for us.

Before you begin, you should know that it is very difficult for any person to change. In general, people tend to feel annoyed if someone else doesn't correct their behaviour after you point it out once or twice. It may make you feel like they are ignoring your advice. If you feel this way, you need some introspection. Ask yourself, 'Am I really trying to change them for their own sake? Is it possible that I want to change them because I dislike their behaviour?'

Try to be prepared to wait for change. If you give advice to someone without expecting a quick change in their behaviour, you won't feel annoyed, even if that person doesn't take your advice and make a change. Because you know that it is extremely difficult for people to change in any way, you can continue to remind them and support their process of change.

You shouldn't become stressed or anxious just because it might seem that they don't listen to you. If your advice was given with their wellbeing in mind rather than for your own benefit, and they choose not to listen, this is their own business. There's no need for you to get upset, or feel any emotion in particular about it. If you become stressed, it means that, although you say (and may even believe), 'I am offering them this advice because changing will be good for them,' in reality, you gave them the advice to fulfil your own needs.

'Your opinion is wrong, you should change it.'

You should not force your thoughts and opinions onto others. You can tell them what you know, but you must ultimately trust others to decide for themselves. You may decide to point out that others are wrong and try to change them, but this leads to conflict. Then, when they don't change, you'll become annoyed: 'He still hasn't come to his senses.' If you think this way and become angry, you are the one who suffers.

If you get angry and annoyed that others are not taking your advice, calmly observe your own mind. Following introspection, if you believe that you truly want to help them to change for their own sake, just give them the necessary information and leave them to decide for themselves. Refrain from trying to reform them in your own way. In this way, the potential that you will be involved in unnecessary conflicts will decrease drastically.

Give-and-Take is a Transaction, Not Love

The expression 'give-and-take' signifies a mutual exchange. The act of giving and taking seems to be fair and natural in personal relationships, but in reality, it is closer to a business transaction. If you consciously do things for other people expecting something in return, you'll likely become unhappy if those expectations are not met. Even when you believe that you're doing something to benefit others, chances are you aren't doing what they truly want, and you may mistakenly overestimate the value of your actions to those people, which inevitably leads to conflict.

Imagine a husband buys an outfit for his wife, and she doesn't seem to appreciate it. He will immediately feel disappointed. He may ask, 'Why don't you wear the outfit that I got for you?' She may answer, 'I don't think it looks good on me.' Then, he may be disappointed or even angry that his gift is not appreciated and respond with something like: 'What? I went to a great deal of trouble to get it for you. Is that all you can say?'

Disappointment and resentment can arise instantly. We can observe how frequently this happens – not just between lovers but also with family and friends.

A woman once consulted me about her feelings of sadness and disappointment in her family: 'I live abroad, far away from my family, so I often call my siblings in Korea. But they never call me, even on special holidays. I want to know how they're doing, but I think to myself, "Why should I be the one to call every time?" So, I haven't called them recently. And they still haven't phoned me. I feel frustrated.' This is like saying, 'What goes around should come around. If I called ten times, they should call me back at least once.'

Many people will empathize with this sentiment. But we are forgetting something important. We call our families because we're concerned about them and want to know how they are doing. That is, we call because we want to call them rather than for their sake. It's not a sin not to call your siblings or your parents. If you want to call them, call them, but if you don't want to call, you don't have to.

Deciding not to call your siblings or parents because they don't return the favour is no different from trying to engage your family in a business transaction. It seems like an unfair deal to you, so you're standing your ground and not calling them. Saying, 'I've done this for you, but what have you done for me?' is no different from wrangling over a business contract. It's not a problem if you do something for others because you want to, but if you wish to receive something in return, your relationship is likely to sour. If your expectation goes unfulfilled, you'll become increasingly disappointed and get into conflict with others. It would be wiser to call your family and frankly express your feelings: 'I feel hurt that I'm the only one to be reaching out to others in the family.'

The reason that conflicts arise among people who are close is because of the desire to receive as much love as one gives. When you love someone, there is a good chance you'll be loved back. But if the love is not reciprocated, or love is not demonstrated in the same way, you may feel very unhappy and betrayed. You may lament, 'Why did I give so much love to someone who wouldn't love me back?'

Here, we must take note that the reason our love leads to hatred and disappointment is not because of the other person, but because of our desire to receive as much as we give, or to receive love in a different way. Thinking, 'I'm doing this for you,' will inevitably lead to a feeling of resentment and the question, 'I go out of my way for you, but what have you done for me?' If you realize that doing things for others is actually for your own happiness, you will not expect anything in return and will naturally not feel any resentment. It's best to refrain from engaging in business-style transactions with your loved ones; instead, you should cultivate genuine meaningful relationships with them.

Life Will Feel Empty
If You Live with a Sense
of Responsibility

They say a parent's love for their child is unconditional and pure. But when times are tough, even parents say things like, 'I've gone through so much to raise you.' This translates to an underlying expectation: 'I've worked hard to raise you, so you owe it to me to take care of me when I'm old.' Believing this, some parents end up resenting their children when life doesn't turn out the way they expect it should have.

If parents fully enjoy the experience of raising their children, they wouldn't feel sad even if their children didn't fulfill any obligations to them once they grew up. Since parenthood already brought them so much joy, it wouldn't even cross their minds that they did anything for their children, or that their children owe them anything. They would simply be happy and grateful when their children get settled and begin their own lives, delighted to see their beloved children grown and independent. When parents subconsciously think, 'I raised you and so you owe me,' they are inevitably setting themselves up to feel disappointed in their children and to bring suffering upon themselves.

I met a man who lived alone while supporting his wife and child, who lived abroad. He came to ask me for advice, saying that even though it was a good decision to send his family away for the sake of his child's education, sometimes his life felt purposeless. 'I am happy that my child is studying overseas, but occasionally, I also feel so empty. How can I free myself from this feeling and become a better father and breadwinner for my family?'

If the purpose of your life seems solely to be the fulfilment of obligations, you may think that you are doing your best, but you are also likely to feel that your entire life is pointless and empty. Asking yourself the question: 'What kind of a parent should I be for my child?' may sound noble, but the hidden meaning behind it is that you are sacrificing yourself for your family, moulding yourself into something to suit them. Over time, this will lead to you becoming stressed and unhappy.

'I'll devote myself to my family.'
'I'll make sacrifices for my children.'

People who say these things have a sense of duty in their hearts. This sense of duty weighs heavily. If you feel burdened, you must ask yourself honestly whether you would like living alone or whether you prefer living together with your family.

If you feel that it is indeed better to be part of your family rather than to live alone, and that it is better to have children no matter how much trouble they may be, you are mistaken if you think you are sacrificing yourself for your partner and children. Rather, you should thank your child, saying 'I'm happy because you're in my life.' To your partner, you should be able to say, 'Although we may sometimes have difficulties, life is better thanks to you.' If you feel grateful to your partner and your children, you will have a happy family life, and you will naturally become a good parent and partner.

Many parents sacrifice their lives to support their adult children, but there is a limit to the sacrifices you should make. Eventually, these people may start to wonder if it is necessary to live this way and ask themselves why they should suffer hardship and remain tied down to a family. Furthermore, if you think you are sacrificing for someone, you'll eventually want to be compensated.

You may think, 'Is that the best you can do when I'm working so hard for you?' As your disappointment grows, you may end up lamenting your fate. Thus, devoting your life to others may prevent you from living a free and happy life.

Being a good parent is no different than being a good partner or spouse. No matter how devoted parents are and how much money they spend on their children, if parents argue their children are more likely to be distressed and to become troubled. If both parents are happy in their marriage, their children are more likely to turn out well. Even those children who don't achieve noteworthy success academically may later grow up to be successful in other ways.

Ultimately, living happily together as a couple is the way to be good parents, so it is better for parents to live peacefully together. Parents living happily together and sending their children to any school, for example, is better than parents living separately and sending their children to a prestigious school. When parents make sacrifices for their children, expectations of their children will increase, so the children end up burdened with these heavy emotions and expectations. As a result, the children's enthusiasm for life may wane somewhat, and they may become overly aware about what their parents may want instead of focussing on what they themselves want for their lives. Even when such children grow up and begin their own families, they may well continue to depend on their parents or continue trying to please their parents instead of becoming truly independent. If you honestly wish for your children's happiness and want to be good parents, you must encourage them to be fully independent by the age of 20 years old.

'I'll feed you, put a roof over your head, and pay for your education until you graduate from school. After that, you are free to live your life as you please.' You could add, 'It doesn't matter to me whether you decide to live alone or get married, and I accept whomever you may wish to marry. Live as your heart desires. We will support your decisions.'

Children will be able to live energetically and adventurously when you set them free to explore the world on their own terms. These days, however, many children are raised within restrained conditions, in restrictive conditions, and most of these children lack spirit and courage. The youth today are generally conservative, seeking only to be secure and avoid challenges, which can have the result of stagnating society as a whole. Children can grow up well anywhere. Parents don't need to worry about them so much. However, if parents have found the experience of raising a child painful and cannot get over this, it will be difficult for the child to become successful. How can a child who brings pain to his parents ever become successful?

If you consider parenting to be a sacrifice, it may feel like a shackle. Let go of thoughts like 'I'm doing all of this for you.' Then, both you and your child can lead happy lives.

Dependence:
the Seed of Resentment

Many people have unrealistic expectations and romantic fantasies about marriage, perhaps because love is such a popular topic for films and fiction. People often assume that if they get married they will be blissfully happy. Such high expectations unfortunately lead to equally large disappointments, so many couples realize that they need to escape their marriages not long after tying the knot.

Instead of thinking of marriage simply as two people living together, people expect to have the kinds of romantic and passionate marital relationships they are used to seeing in films or reading about in books. They become unhappy when their spouses don't shower them with undivided attention and love. They may have experienced heart-fluttering moments when they were dating, but after marriage, they begin to find being with each other a little more dull, and realize that they don't actually have as much to talk about as they used to. Even though their spouses are neither bad nor significantly lacking, they may complain, saying, 'We don't talk as much as we used to when we were dating, and things are a bit boring now. I didn't think this is how a marriage would be...'

Cooked rice has no special flavour, but it's good for your health. Alternatively, fast food might taste good, but it is bad your health.

A woman once asked me for advice because she felt distressed by her obsession over her husband: 'I don't know how to let go of my desire to rely and depend on my husband. I'm afraid that if I let go of it, I may start obsessing over my children instead.'

Obsessive attachment comes from dependence. From a positive perspective, depending on someone means trusting that person. From a negative perspective, it is servility, because our joys and sorrows depend almost entirely on the other person's actions. You mistake it for love and attention, but it's actually a state of obsessive attachment. Those with a tendency to attach obsessively may also shift this attention from one 'object' to another. If you can't let go of your obsession over your husband, but you shun him because you are hurt by something, the object of your obsession may shift to your children instead. This is very burdensome for your children and will be a source of future conflict with them.

One positive aspect of a marriage is that spouses provide companionship for each other, to ease their loneliness. But when spouses are overly dependent on each other, their marriage becomes a burden and can even feel like a prison keeping them trapped inside. Rather than the marriage itself, it is the state of over dependence which confines the husband and wife.

In general, those who feel that they were not sufficiently or appropriately loved by their parents might be more likely than others to fall easily for anyone who shows them even a little attention. They may be hungry for the love they feel they didn't receive from their parents, and so seek it instead from a love interest or a spouse.

Initially, it may seem like the love they missed out on as children is being fulfilled by the marriage. But with time, they will gradually grow disappointed and resentful toward their spouses. They then turn to their children in an attempt to satisfy their hunger for the love that was not satisfied by their parents or spouses.

Unfortunately, it is likely that they will be disappointed by their children as well. As a result, they end up resenting their parents, despising their spouses, and feeling betrayed by their children. At this point, they may feel like everything is wrong with their lives. They started off by resenting their parents, and while wandering through life in search of a person to replace what they felt they were missing, they also ended up despising their spouses and children along the way.

Being dependent on another person means that your life changes course based on the attitudes and actions of that person – this is sure to create suffering. It is like tying yourself up with several ropes, then handing the end of one to your parents, the end of another to your spouse, one to each of your friends, and the rest to your children – then instructing them all to pull. Inevitably, you will be dragged in whichever direction they pull you.

If you allow your own direction to be at the mercy of others in this way, you end up losing sight of your own perspective, judgement and sense of autonomy. Being trapped and tethered to those around you in this way, confusion and distress are inevitable – you will not have control over your own life.

Generally, our idea of love includes the tendency to say that we depend on the person we love. But true love means loving others while remaining independent. Be ready to provide help and refuge to those whom you love without expecting anything in return. If we make sacrifices for those we love because we expect something in return, we will inevitably end up resentful and disillusioned.

We rarely become enemies with strangers. Most often we run into problems with those we have been close to if our expectations of them (and our dependence on them) turn our love into resentment. Starting today, make a conscious effort to break your habit of depending on others and imprisoning yourself and others in the name of love. Instead embrace this mindset: 'I am in charge of my own life.'

Stop Interfering
in Other People's Lives

Sometimes our concern for other people – especially those close to us – becomes excessive, to the point that we begin to interfere in their lives. We often use our status as a parent, child or relative as the justification for such interference. We meddle in their affairs, thinking that we are helping, but it is likely that the other person may feel burdened by our behaviour. Rather than helping, our eagerness to assist can bring suffering to both ourselves and to others. A woman who was worried about her unmarried, unemployed children once asked me for advice: 'My son and daughter are both in their thirties. Although they have been job-hunting for years, neither has managed to get a job. They've been trying very hard, so I can't understand why they haven't succeeded. On top of that, neither is married. I'm very concerned about them. What should I do?'

It is not unusual for parents to worry about their children. They think, 'She should find a good job,' or 'He should get married soon.' These parents are just expressing their concern for their children, but the children often find such expectations burdensome. After your child reaches the age of 20, you should let them manage their own affairs, whether work or relationships. I'm not telling you to stop loving your children; you should just stop interfering in their lives.

When I give this type of advice, some people reply, 'But isn't that being uncaring and apathetic?' Others ask whether this contradicts the Buddha's teachings, which instruct us to love and look after all living beings. When I tell people to refrain from interfering in others' lives, I'm not advising them to be indifferent toward their families or the world. What I mean is that they should respect their children and start seeing them as independent and autonomous individuals, capable of making their own decisions and finding their own way.

Of course, all children need to be cared for. Throughout their preschool, primary school and secondary school years, children must be nurtured and carefully guided. Parents are responsible for taking care of their own children. If there is a child without biological parents, another adult should step in and take on the role of caregiver. Regardless of blood relationships, every child deserves to be cared for by responsible adults.

As children grow older and reach adolescence, they change physically, emotionally and mentally. At the same time, their sense of individuality strengthens and they crave greater independence. Where they might have once followed their parents' instructions without question, they begin to become more assertive. Teenagers become interested in doing things that parents would prefer they didn't, while resisting doing what their parents ask of them. So, conflicts arise between parents and their teenage children. This is quite natural, all part of growing up.

During adolescence, children begin to make their own decisions and have different experiences. In the process, they make mistakes, endure disappointments and heartaches, and get hurt – all of these experiences help them mature. Although parents may worry, they should stand back and give their children space. This is true love. If parents continue interfering in their children's lives, in addition to causing conflicts, they will rob their children of many opportunities to grow through their own experiences. As children grow into adulthood, parents must relinquish their attachment. This is the only way that children can mature to become fully independent.

Parents should be neither overly involved with, nor completely indifferent toward, their children. They should love their children but only provide support when it is requested.

Careful advice offered in response to a request yields positive results.

However, unsolicited advice is rarely received well and often has negative results.

If I offered too much unsolicited advice, people would be loathed to come see me at all when they are actually facing difficulties, let alone ask me for help. Instead, they would think, 'I wonder what Sunim will scold me about this time?' Thus, unsolicited advice has many adverse and unintended effects.

If you have an uncaring attitude – 'Do whatever you want. I don't care,' – when others don't listen to you, this will further compound the problem. Both providing unsolicited advice and withholding help when it is requested will undermine the trust people have in you. Neither interference nor indifference is helpful to others. Sometimes we think, 'Should I leave her alone to work it out?' or 'Should I correct him?' These kinds of thoughts come from our desire to interfere. You may want to help, but if the other person wants to try to do something on their own, it's best to wait and allow them the time and space they need.

The same principles apply to romantic relationships. When you have strong feelings for someone, you may want to offer them unsolicited help. This behaviour arises from ignorance. If you want your interest to be reciprocated, you must refrain from acting on impulse, and instead be able to observe patiently. True love is waiting until your loved one actually needs or requests help.

It is generally good to help those in need, but there are things you must bear in mind. Remember it is better to provide help to others when they actually need it. If you help others because you feel they need help, you may bring trouble upon yourself. Also, blaming yourself for not being able to help those in need will only make you unhappy. It is good to help when you can, but if you can't, that's fine too. Do not easily assume that you can help or teach others – it is easy to fall into the trap of trying to help out of self-interest, or to show off, or to make yourself feel good. If you are trying to comfort a person who is dealing with a difficult situation, and you observe your own mind carefully, it is likely you will find that you are actually motivated by self-interest. If you really want to help, you must first listen to the other person attentively, and then share any relevant experiences or thoughts you may have had.

Trying to impose your views on other people's lives only creates unnecessary tension and trouble for yourself. Whether your focus is your parents, partner, friends, siblings or children, once you start meddling in their lives, your own life will become exhausting. If you feel drained from helping others, it means that your desire to interfere in other peoples' lives has outstripped your ability to actually provide them with help. This is a sign that you need to take a step back and let everyone live their own lives. Rather than giving unsolicited assistance, wait until it is requested, and then provide help in the best way you can. That way, you will be helpful to others and will enjoy a more leisurely life yourself.

All the Trees Together Make a Forest

When you go to the mountains, do you find only one kind of tree or many different kinds of trees? You'll see broadleaf trees as well as pine trees. You can even find smaller trees sheltering beneath the taller trees. Amidst the diversity and differences, they all grow together harmoniously.

Noticing the way nature works like this, we may question why conflicts arise between people who get married because they love each other. Do they argue because of the bad habits of one person? Do conflicts happen because of the complaints of the other person? These are not the true sources of conflict. When one partner does what they like, and the other asks, 'Why do you do this all the time? It's bad for your health and wastes money. How can you do something so stupid?' the first may well become frustrated. Conflicts arise when partners antagonize each other in this way.

It all comes down to this assumption: 'I'm right. You're wrong.' This inevitably leads to conflict. Humankind is as diverse as the trees in all the forests of the world. Our thoughts and preferences are as diverse as people's physical appearances.

To live in harmony, we need to acknowledge our differences. You may want to go out, but your partner might want to stay in. You might like someone, but that person might not like you. Everyone sees things from their own point of view. When we insist that our own perspectives are correct and all others are wrong, we can't avoid friction. We fight because we mistakenly think others are wrong, when they are merely different.

If people think of themselves as the centre of the universe and try to measure others against their own subjective standards, even married couples are bound to fight. If we recognize and understand each other's differences, we should be able to avoid conflict, even if we were to move in with someone we just met that same day passing on the street.

Imagine if an employer and employee properly understood each other's perspectives right from the beginning of their working relationship. The employee would realize, 'I guess my boss needs to save on labour costs.' The employer might think, 'I am sure my employee would like to be paid a little bit more.' Each could understand the other in this way. This is not necessarily the same as agreeing with one another. If each understood the other, there would be room for negotiation and a willingness to engage.

If somebody insults you, it's difficult to listen while retaining your sense of humour. But imagine if someone started talking in his sleep and said, 'I can't stand Pomnyun Sunim.' What would I do? Would I get angry, wake him up, grab him by the collar and yell, 'What did you just say to me?' I wouldn't do that. I would just laugh and say, 'Wow, he talks a lot in his sleep.' Interpersonal friction caused by differences in opinion isn't very different from talking in your sleep. In both cases, people are caught up in their own thoughts, and they're not able to rid themselves of ignorance. When we understand this, we can smile and let it go. Effort to understand other people must take priority over any effort to make them change their behaviour. If it would benefit people to improve themselves, it is better to provide them with the opportunity to realize this on their own rather than pointing it out before they are ready to hear it. For example, your spouse might refuse to do any work around the house. If you understood them, you might think,

'That's all right,' or 'At least they work hard at their job.' If you believe that they need to help with housework in order to set a good example for the children, there are some things you could try. You could ask for help by saying, 'Honey, I feel too tired to get out of bed. Could you get me a cup of coffee?' If you were to abruptly demand, 'Why do I always make the coffee? You make it this time!' you'd be much more likely to start an argument. Rather, you could create an opportunity for them to help out by explaining the problem and then asking whether they would help to solve it.

It's extremely difficult to change someone. Adjusting yourself to the other person is the quickest and least painful solution to most issues. If you seek to change someone despite knowing that people don't change easily, you will need a lot of affection and wisdom. Instead of forcefully trying to change someone who doesn't want to be changed, you need to learn how to encourage change with wisdom and gentleness.

If you feel unhappy in your relationship with others, try changing your point of view. Notice their good points, rather than their shortcomings. When you make an effort to view others in a positive way, you will notice more positive things about them for which you can be thankful, and you will be one step closer to happiness.

Part 04

We Need to Revise the Definition of Happiness

Our current society is extremely competitive. People commonly believe, 'I can only survive by defeating someone else.' As people jostle for power, positions and money, there is bound to be more conflict and strife. People think they will be happy when they win and unhappy when they lose. Therefore, everyone tries to become a winner by defeating others.

However, this so-called happiness is fundamentally built on the foundations of others' defeat. While we rejoice at passing an exam, others may be devastated because they failed it. While we are delighted to support the winning side in an election, others are despairing due to their loss. While we celebrate making a successful bid, others will be upset to have lost the deal.

There are people who have stable, high-paying jobs at big corporations. But at the same time, there are many with temporary, low-paying jobs. Also, there are many unable to find a job who are suffering because of unemployment.

However, we blindly run on in our lives thinking, 'I'm okay, as long as this doesn't happen to me.'

But what is waiting for us at the end of this track we rush along like racehorses?

What is True Success?

Everyone dreams of a successful life. Then, what is true success? A 27-year-old man came to talk to me, and said: 'My criteria for success have been changing every year. Two years ago, I thought I would feel successful if I earned an annual salary of more than $30,000. A year ago, I became a tax accountant and now I'm preparing for the final exam. My current focus for success is passing this exam. My question is this: What is true success in life?'

I asked him a question in return. 'Is passing the exam a success and not passing the exam a failure? What are you going to do if you fail?'

'I will to continue to study, and take the exam again.'

'Why do you want to be successful?'

'I want to make money.'

'Why do you want to make money?'

'To live an easier life, I think.'
'What is an easy life?'
'Living in a big house.'
'It will be difficult to maintain a big house.'
'But I want to live like wealthy people do.'
'Why do you want to live in a big house? Do you like showing off?'
'Yes, to some extent.'
'What is good about showing off a big house?'
'Well, I guess there's really nothing good about showing it off.'

As you can see from this dialogue, many people work hard to succeed, but when they're asked why they want to succeed, their answers are often vague. If I continue to press them for an answer, they say, 'To be happy.'

That's right. Ultimately, we want to be happy and free. But what if we waste so much time chasing happiness that we die without ever experiencing it?

This young man said that his criteria for success was to pass the exam for which he'd been preparing. If he is studying to achieve a goal, he should be happy about the process of studying itself. However, we suffer while studying and think that we succeed only if we pass the exam at the end. The process of hiking up the mountain should make us happy, but we suffer in the process of climbing up and feel happy only when we reach the top of the mountain. Is it a failure if we fail to reach the top? No. If we reach only half-way up the mountain, we have achieved that much.

Still, we run ahead with all our strength without thinking about where we're going. What kind of success are we working so hard to achieve?

One day, a doctor said he was worried because he didn't have many patients. So, I said, 'Should people get sick so that you can make money?'

How can he be a genuine doctor when he wants people to be sick? These days, many people seem to want to become doctors, not because they want to help make people well, but because they want to make money. Some doctors are even suspected of over-diagnosing and over-treating patients in order to increase their profit.

The situation is similar with lawyers. Since it's hard for lawyers to make money working for marginalized people who are not well protected by the law, they flock to large law firms that make money by helping huge companies evade taxes. This is because their goal is to make money. Why do people waste their precious talent to become slaves to money? Is that true success?

The world is crazy about money, and the only religion people truly believe in seems to be money. As the world revolves around money, people are likely to betray the trust of others if they can see a chance of making money. For instance, some people may leave their partners for wealthier people. People don't hesitate to leave the company they worked at for over 30 years to move to another company that is able to offer them a higher salary. They may seem clever for doing this, but in reality they are actually just enslaved by their pursuit of money.

For people to become happier, we need to revise the definition of success. A doctor's duty is to treat patients. A good doctor is someone who heals people who are ill. A doctor's ultimate goal should be to have no patients. A good lawyer should help clients to work things out and find solutions to difficult situations. When your goal is people's happiness rather than money, your life can be deemed successful.

Most people think that making a lot of money and living in a big home in a large city is the sign of a successful life. But success depends on what makes you happy. If you live on a farm in the countryside, you may be satisfied with your life and think, 'I'm so happy to be free to do the work I want while enjoying the fresh air.' This would mean that your life is successful.

However, since people have so many misconceptions about success, they live their lives trying to meet other people's standards. Others might view them as successful, but they're in danger of becoming mentally exhausted. That's why, when people are old or sick, they may feel that their life's accomplishments were futile rather than worthwhile. I'm not saying that people shouldn't study or work hard. What I mean is that people shouldn't waste their lives on pursuing false success, because later, when they look back on their lives, they may regret it.

True success starts with knowing that each moment of your life is valuable and precious. No matter what situation you're in, you should be able to enjoy your life under the given circumstances. So, you need to constantly check whether you are happy in the present moment.

If we can maintain such a perspective, we can lead a life that was successful yesterday, is successful today, and will be successful tomorrow.

Do Not Build Your Happiness on Other People's Misfortune

Many people's goal in life is to become successful. Generally, it is assumed that being successful involves graduating from a good college, getting a good job, marrying well, and so on. Graduating from a prestigious university is supposedly key in finding a good job. A good job is supposedly one that has a light workload, pays well, offers good benefits, gives you some authority, and is well-regarded by others. In short, being successful is measured as having more wealth, status, prestige and popularity than most others around you. Of course, when we define success in such a frank manner, some might disagree.

Usually, people don't consider whether their success has been achieved through harm caused to others. Unfortunately, that is the truth. If you live in an apartment that is 2,000 square feet (185 square metres), and people around you call you rich, this means that it is likely they live in a smaller apartment, and they may even envy your home. Their admiration might make you happy, it may even make you feel that you are successful. But they are likely envious of your circumstances, suffering as they wish that they also had what you have.

Most people think that simply having more of anything than others, whether it be money, power, property, or fame, is the key to a successful life. They think that having more will also enable them to be generous to others later. That is, they think they'll be able to donate more, give more to their church or temple, establish a charity, and do worthwhile things that mean they will be remembered as having made a positive difference to the world.

The problem is that 'having more' is a relative concept. For you to have 'more' than others, there needs to be someone else who has 'less' than you. Let's use wealth as an example. For someone to work less and earn more, another person must work more and be paid less.

The same goes for power. If there is someone giving an order, there must be someone available to receive and respond to the order. For one person to succeed, others must fail; the greater the wealth of one individual, the greater the number of people who can't even afford to satisfy their basic needs.

In the end, the success so many of us pursue is fundamentally achieved by passing suffering to others. Today's society seems to be structured in such a way that achieving success is almost always only possible by sacrificing others. One's success inevitably requires another person's failure, so it is not realistically possible for everyone to succeed together. This is because our society currently consists of a pyramid structure where one person's gain is only possible because of someone else's loss. People jostle to seize the top spot, and when a few secure those coveted spots up high, the majority of others are relegated to positions that support them.

Even if the top-level positions are filled with very smart people, the pyramid will crumble without many more people filling the middle and bottom positions to provide structure and support. The few people on top are only able to rise to these positions because the people underneath them function as stepping stones and scaffolding.

However, those at the top often take their privilege for granted, believing that they achieved such giddy heights because they are more deserving, more intelligent, more capable than others. They may even dismiss those supporting them from below as less competent or less diligent than themselves. Thus, most people reserve their highest admiration for higher-ranking positions and correspondingly seek to improve their own position at almost any cost.

In a society like this, it's easy for those who satisfy their own desires at all costs to be lauded as examples of success. These days, those who work hard for their communities rather than just themselves, and who care about others, are often dismissed as being naive, while those who live idly and thoughtlessly after simply receiving inherited money are envied and considered lucky.

When there are people around you who are suffering, but you have more money, power, and prestige than others, the pleasure you derive from your privilege is won at the cost of others' sacrifices. Therefore, you must realize that you're able to work less (or perhaps not at all) while still living in comfort because there are people who work much harder but earn considerably less, and still live in poverty.

One day, King Prasenasit asked the Buddha, 'How do I become a great king?' And the Buddha answered,

What is Happiness?

'Love your subjects as you would love your only son. You mustn't build your happiness on other people's misfortune. Do not regard the position of a king as something special. If you always help the poor and the sick and comfort the lonely, you don't need to leave home and lead the ascetic life of a monk. If a king is foolish, it is difficult to preserve his own life, much less a whole country.'

In general, we think that a great leader should be powerful. But the Buddha emphasized that King Prasenasit should not consider himself something special because of his position as king, telling him that caring for the people is the most important part of being a leader.

As the prince of a kingdom, the Buddha had led a life of luxury. But after witnessing the suffering of the common people, he stepped out of his enviable life as though it was nothing more than an old shoe, and he left home. When he made this decision, the Buddha decided not to follow the path of taking away others' possessions to fill his own storehouse, or of achieving his own success by diminishing someone else. He did not take away another's honour to gain his own.

But somehow we have mistakenly come to believe that succeeding in life requires building foundations for our own happiness on the misfortunes of others. We have pursued this direction blindly, thinking this is the only path to our own happiness. Moving forward, what do we truly need to do so that everyone can become happy together? Even though we live in a competitive society, how do we win without oppressing others, and lose without feeling defeated? The answer is simple: reset your life goals so you consider coming second rather than first to be a success. For example, if there is an opportunity for a promotion, look to your colleague and wish for them to get promoted ahead of you. Some may struggle to process this, wondering, 'Won't I lag behind in life if I do that?' But actually no, you won't.

What I'm trying to say is that you should refrain from obsessing over getting the promotion, for example. I'm not saying that you shouldn't work hard at your job. You should work very hard, but when there is an opportunity for promotion or reward, give way to others.

For example, let's say you went somewhere to sell products your company creates, and a competitor showed up to show their products. Telling the customer to consider your competitor's products first is not entirely for the sake of the competitor. Rather, it is for your own sake. If you are genuinely relaxed about the customer considering both offerings, you won't be stressed by the competition, regardless of whatever choice the customer makes. You won't feel defeated if the customer ends up buying your competitor's product instead of yours, and should the customer choose to purchase your product (even after you have been gracious about your competitor's product), that is their choice; you didn't have to trample on your competitor. However, if you can't adopt this altruistic attitude and feel compelled to compete against others, you will encounter the consequences. If you trample on your competitor today, someday they will reciprocate. No one can hide from the consequences of their actions, and you will suffer less if you can accept the consequences willingly and so avoid feeling resentful or victimized.

If we are awakened to how life works, we can become successful, have a comfortable life, and also make money. However, we lead weary lives because we try to defeat others at any cost, without understanding how the world really works. If you don't have the addiction to winning, you have no need to be nervous or anxious no matter who you encounter. You'll be at ease no matter what you do and where you live, and you'll be able to get along easily with everyone.

Desire is Like a Burning Log

The capitalism that dominates the world we live in today is excellent at fuelling human desires – and there is an immense problem with this system. Capitalism not only fulfills our desires but encourages them to perpetually grow. It seems our appetites can never be satisfied.

Back in the days when South Korea experienced food shortages, people who could afford to eat beef soup with white rice were considered well-off. When food became abundant, having good quality clothes became a sign of wealth. As affluence increased, so people's standards of affluence expanded, from eating good food to wearing certain clothes, to owning a car, to owning a house, and so on. People's desires continued to grow.

Even though people now enjoy more material abundance than ever before, they also want to own more things than ever before. We have so much, yet we still have a tendency to feel dissatisfied and think we need more, comparing ourselves endlessly with others. People are neither happier nor more generous than they were when they barely had anything. In fact, many have become more cold-hearted while competing to have more.

Moreover, South Koreans are obsessed with economic growth. Since the country has recorded steady economic growth during the past fifty years, people panic if the growth rate plateaus or decreases even slightly. This is because a preoccupation with working hard to bring about economic growth and to improve people's material lives, which began when South Korea was poor, still persists.

The truth is that however bad the current economic situation in South Korea may seem, people now lead far more affluent lives than they would have 20 years ago. However, people also complain more, are more dissatisfied, and are generally less happy. This is because our expectations of material wealth and economic status have also increased. With such a relative definition of success, it's no wonder that the feeling of deprivation endures, no matter how much the economy grows.

We now need to come to our senses and learn to live frugally. If we continue indulging ourselves in material consumption as we do now, what do you think will happen to the Earth?

This kind of human desire cannot ever be satisfied. Whenever a desire is fulfilled, it only grows bigger. For example, even if you have always walked to school, once you get used to travelling there by car, you may well come to prefer driving and won't want to walk to school anymore. Once we get used to more convenience and comfort in our lives, it becomes difficult to return to the old ways.

As we allow our desires more and more control, they take charge of our lives. When a desire is fulfilled, we temporarily feel elated with happiness. We think that the more we have, the freer and happier we will be.

A college student once asked me for advice because she was worried that she might have a shopping addiction: 'I think I spend far more money than my peers. I have a part-time job just to earn enough money for shopping. As I spend most of the money I earn, I get anxious if my income decreases even just a little bit, although I still earn just as much as my friends. I feel inferior if I can't spend as much money as I usually do. I'm worried that I feel this way when I'm still quite young.'

First and foremost, the fact that this young woman has become aware that she is addicted to shopping and feels she has a problem means that she is unhappy living the way she does now. It's fine if shopping makes her feel happy and free. However, if she can't stop shopping even when she feels worried about it and trapped by it, this means she is addicted. For now, she holds on to the addiction because the amount of suffering it brings is still bearable. But soon, the time will come when she has no other choice but to quit or risk damage to her life.

As for me, when I'm invited to a big house, I look around and think, 'Oh my, it must be tough to clean.' But if you can't let go of the habit of perceiving bigger as better, you'll continue to want newer and bigger things. Eventually, you will try to satisfy your desire even if you can't afford to and end up having to borrow to pay for it.

If you feel nervous, anxious, or chronically dissatisfied with life, you're more susceptible to developing an addiction. You can't control your desire to shop, and you want to spend increasingly more money. To do that, you need to make more money so you may keep changing your job to find roles that pay more. At this point, you have essentially become a slave to money. When your addiction grows, you begin to take risks to make even more money. You tell yourself, 'This is just a one-off,' even though it worries you to take the risk. Further down the road, you may even be tempted to take part in illegal activities if they pay significantly better than your usual salary.

Initially, almost no one who gets involved in illegal or unethical activity plans to carry on with it long-term. People think, 'I'll just do it this once,' because they have an urgent need for money at that particular time. Once they make a sizable amount of money, they think they'll be set for a while and so they can stop taking the risks, but it doesn't work out that way. As the money they gain increases, their desire to spend increases even faster.

Such risks lurk in a shopping addiction. Therefore, instead of waiting until you reach a dead end, you must quit the moment you recognize that you have a problem.

As your addiction takes hold, it will alter the way you think. Then, you'll begin to deceive yourself. It's almost impossible to detect the changes that you go through yourself. Therefore, you must quit as soon as you have recognized the problem.

Hunters know that a jackrabbit will take bait more readily in the winter than in the summer because food is scarcer when the weather is cold. People are no different. When they're caught in a desire for something scarce, like large amounts of money, there is a high chance that they will seek to fulfil this desire without realizing that they are risking a great loss, just like a hungry rat taking the poisonous bait. In other words, food is a weakness to hungry people, bribery has power over those who want wealth, and flattery works on those who long to be admired.

When you're blinded by greed, you are unable to make good choices. In order to make the right choice, you must give up on satisfying your desire to a certain degree, but instead you rush forwards, focused only on the carrot dangling ahead.

Stop and look around to check where you are and where you're heading. Make sure you are not hurtling blindly toward the edge of a cliff in your quest to satisfy your hunger.

Three Levels of Want: Need, Desire and Greed

People are happy when their needs are satisfied. We feel good if we're doing something we want to do. We're satisfied when everything turns out the way we hoped it would. We feel happy when we accomplish what we want to but miserable when we do not.

These feelings of happiness and unhappiness all stem from wants and needs. There are endless kinds of wants and needs, such as needing to eat, wanting to wear nice clothes, needing shelter, wanting to have material possessions, wanting to win, and so forth. But realistically, it is impossible to satisfy one's every need and want. Take a family for example. If every member of the household did whatever they wanted, whenever they wanted to, the family couldn't function. All members of the family would suffer. Thus, pursuing your desire can ultimately cause great harm to others as well as to yourself.

However, a need or a want in and of itself is not necessarily all bad. Everyone has needs, and sometimes they can be helpful if we harness them correctly. But it is important to understand the boundaries.

There are three types of needs and wants. The first type is physiological needs. These basic human needs include seeking food when hungry, drinking when thirsty, sleeping when tired, the ability to warm up when cold, and having ways to cool down when hot. Because one's survival is threatened if these basic needs are not met, an individual has the right to satisfy these needs, and society must also ensure that its members are able to fulfil these basic needs.

Next, there are relative needs, which are wants or desires. The desire to eat something more delicious, to own more than others, to achieve higher status, to wear better clothes, to live in a more comfortable environment – these are all relative needs. These desires arise in people because of comparing themselves to others. Such desires do not have a defining boundary; there is no end to how far they might go. Therefore, these desires should be restrained, since they can never be fully satisfied despite all the time and effort people spend chasing them. It is important to have some degree of control over our desires, and societies have regulations which serve to constrain individual desires to some extent.

Finally, there are excessive needs, which can also be referred to as greed. Overeating might satisfy your appetite or your desire for a certain taste or texture, but it is bad for your health. Both drinking too much and overworking to make more money stem from greed – it can do great harm. Individuals must learn to protect themselves by letting go of greed, and society must regulate the greed of individuals in order to protect itself and keep everything functioning as it should.

Satisfying needs is not only important to individuals but also to society as a whole. Society must provide appropriate safeguards to manage the fulfillment of needs. From an individual's perspective, fulfilling survival needs is a basic right, and everyone should be able to exercise that right. However, the process of satisfying individuals' relative needs/desires must be regulated as they are impossible to ever fully satisfy. Individuals must free themselves from their desires to satisfy excessive needs or greed.

Certain physiological needs must be met as basic human rights, and society must ensure that everyone can meet their survival needs. Desires and wants, on the other hand, should be allowed to some degree but at the same time restrained appropriately, and greed must be deterred through proper regulation.

A man I spoke with said that he wanted to live frugally, but he had trouble putting this into practice: 'In the past, I pursued a life of wealth and success. After listening to your Dharma talks, I have begun to think that I would like to lead a frugal life. However, when I think realistically about how to make a living and get married, which would require me to purchase a car and a house, I feel I should save a lot of money, so I start obsessing about money again.'

If you always ate everything you wanted, would that be beneficial or harmful to your health? We consume food to give us energy and to keep our bodies healthy, but often, food that is pleasing to the palate isn't necessarily healthy. There are foods that taste good but can harm the body, and there are foods that we might find less palatable that are of benefit to the body. If you want to be healthy, sometimes you should refrain from eating unhealthy foods you might be craving, and other times you should choose to eat foods you know are good for you even if you don't particularly feel like eating them at that time. Food consumption should be focused on maintaining your health rather than pleasing your palate. The same goes for wearing clothes. The purpose of wearing clothes is to protect our bodies. We dress to stay warm in cold weather and to stay cool and protect our skin when the sun is blazing. Those who wear expensive designer clothes are often overly concerned about their clothes. In fact, they value their clothes more for how they look than the protection or comfort they offer. Such people may well end up becoming slaves to their wardrobes.

A similar idea may be applied to the house that we live in. A larger house takes up more space and holds increasingly more furniture and valuables; the bigger and more expensive your house and belongings, the more likely it is that you will end up protecting your home rather than being protected by it. The house becomes the master, and you become the servant. When we blindly follow the desire for 'more and better' possessions, we may end up losing control of our lives before we even realize what is happening.

If we are not careful, one day we may find ourselves living lives of servitude to all kinds of material things like clothing, food, houses, and so on. You must maintain awareness to prevent your desires from taking control of your life.

Wanting to make money through employment or business isn't bad, and it's not greedy as such. However, it's important to live modestly no matter how much money you make. Living frugally will enable you to save money. If you eat modestly, refrain from buying expensive clothing, and use public transport, your monthly spending will likely be only about half of what your friends spend.

I am not saying that you should be a cheapskate. I'm just recommending that you avoid unnecessary spending. If you live modestly, your savings for the future will increase.

Live your life based on a clear value system of your own instead of chasing standards set by other people. If you think you can get by without purchasing a car, you can walk or use public transport even if others are travelling by car. You don't need to buy a car simply because everyone else has one. Furthermore, when planning to get married, you should first find out whether your prospective spouse shares your values of living modestly. If this is important to you, it should be important to the person you marry as well if you are to have a peaceful life together.

If you marry someone who has different values and is more extravagant than you, you will have to please that person throughout your life together. It is likely you would have to pretend you're wealthy (or at least that you want to be) and you may even need to behave falsely in order to attract that person.

If you do this, you will be inviting disaster. Therefore, if you want to live according to your principles, you should marry someone who shares your life values. If you fail to meet someone compatible, you can opt not to get married. That way, you can avoid choosing a job solely based on the money you will earn, and you can avoid spending your life chasing ways to make more money. This will free you to be in control of your own life and do what you want to do.

You can live your life as you please in accordance with your values. However, because we live in a world full of other people, there are a few rules that we should adhere to:

- » First, people can live their lives as they see fit, but no one has the freedom to cause harm to another – one should not harm or kill others.
- » Second, people have the right to pursue their own interests, but they don't have the right to infringe on other people's interests. One should not extort valuables or steal from others.
- » Third, people have the right to love and to be happy, but they don't have the right to harass others. One should not sexually abuse, intimidate or assault others.
- » Fourth, people have the right to speak freely, but they do not have the right to hurt others with words. One should not swear or lie.
- » Fifth, people have the right to drink alcohol but not to get drunk and distress others. Therefore, one should not get intoxicated.

Other than these five rules, everyone can live their lives as they please.

You might say that all this sounds simple enough. However, the problem is that these days people have fewer children, and parents are now so indulgent and protective of their children that they fail to teach them basic ethics early on. These days teachers have to deal with incidents of violence and other problems at school, including stealing, deceit and sexual harassment – these all fall under the five rules outlined above.

Some parents adopt a vaguely permissive attitude to their children's bad behaviour, even when it causes harm or loss to others. They fear that any kind of punishment will dishearten their child. However, they also insist that poor grades and bad exam results are unacceptable. Thus, children may come to believe that poor academic performance is worse than causing harm or loss to others.

Therefore, both at home and in society, we should establish meaningful and logical standards for reasonable behaviour and controlling desires. We must teach these rules to our children. This is something we all need to do to coexist successfully in this world.

The Individual is the Seed and Society is the Field

In my Dharma Q&A talks, I consistently emphasize the importance of an individual's attitude and mindset. During one of these talks, an attendee objected and said: 'You've said that, as each of us strives to change ourselves, the world gradually transforms through the accumulation of our individual efforts. While this is a nice idea, surely exclusive focus on individual self-reflection leaves a lot to be desired. Flaws in the social system can cause such a lot of human suffering, pain and sacrifice. As systemic injustices become more entrenched, the world is growing increasingly worse, so surely it's not right to emphasize change on an individual level without questioning the validity and effectiveness of the existing systems. The systems aren't working. So why is it that those exploiting the system for their own gain at the expense of others do not reflect on themselves?'

No matter what circumstances we find ourselves in, we must carry on living. This doesn't mean that we should unconditionally accept unfairness in the world. As long as we're alive, we must continue striving to make the world a better place for everyone to live. However, society cannot be changed quickly or easily. That's why we must be able to accept current circumstances while simultaneously working to improve them.

I emphasize the importance of individual attitude and mindset because we have a strong tendency to blame the behaviour and external circumstances of others, rather than taking responsibility and thinking about what we can do on a personal level. Most of us seek happiness outside of ourselves. For example, we think that we'll be happier if our child gets better grades, if our spouse cuts back on their drinking, if our parents stop offering us unsolicited advice, or if the world changes. However, does my desire for change in others actually cause them to change? No. Does complaining about the world make it a better place? No, it doesn't. Does this mean that I have no other choice but to suffer? No, not at all.

By changing my frame of mind, I can find freedom and happiness, regardless of my circumstances. That's why I tell people to refrain from blaming others. When we take control of our own lives, we become freer and happier.

A handful of beans was scattered in an arid field full of gravel, and two of them grew to become sprouts. In situations like this, it's common for people to say, 'Look, those that are strong enough to survive have found a way regardless.' If a similar handful of beans was sown in a fertile field, and every one of them survived except two, people would say, 'Look, those that are not fit to survive die.'

They are saying that whether a seed sprouts or not depends only on the seed itself. However, if only 2 per cent of seeds sown in a field of gravel sprouted, but 98 per cent sprouted in a fertile field, this means that the quality of the field also affects the seeds' rates of survival.

For farming to be successful, it is not enough to simply have good seeds. The field must also be fertile. In the context of our lives, the seed is the individual, and the field is our society. Individual practice can be compared to making a good seed. Enriching the field can be compared to creating a good society.

When individuals are happy and social conditions are conducive, we can become truly happy.

Cultivating a society rooted in justice and general welfare is not a separate issue from ensuring individual happiness.

Every January, I lead a Buddhist pilgrimage of hundreds of people to India. We all take the same bus, stay at the same hotels, and eat at the same restaurants. Despite travelling under the same conditions, I always find some people smiling the whole time, while others look extremely unhappy. When we get on a very uncomfortable truck, there's always someone who thinks it's fun and says, 'Where else would I be able to ride a truck like this? What an experience!' Inevitably another person will complain and say something like, 'How can anyone in the modern world still need to travel like this?'

People's moods can change depending on their environment. The way you feel in a smoke-filled, noisy place is different from the way you feel surrounded by nature, out in the fresh air, near clean water. The level of happiness you feel can differ based on your surroundings.

When we can't change the environment, we still have the option to adapt our frame of mind, to become happier than the previous day. This is practice. For example, you may have complained to your spouse about their drinking on and off for 20 years, but to no avail.

So maybe you change the way you think about the issue, deciding, 'Well, go ahead – you drink as much as you like.' You will find that you feel less annoyed. Your spouse may drink just as much, but you will be more content based on your new mindset.

The root cause of your spouse's drinking may lie in the fact that no matter how hard they work, they are unable to improve their economic status. The problem may stem from socio-structural factors. In this situation, although it is important to feel compassion instead of resentment, it's also important to take a step further and work towards social changes that may reduce their stress levels and so diminish their need to drink quite so much.

In current society, there is extreme disparity between the rich and the poor. The vast majority of people – those of us not included in the highly-wealthy, hugely-privileged class – are having an increasingly difficult time making ends meet. Quality of life is diminishing, and at the same time an increased number of people are suffering from relative poverty.

The situation will only improve when economic polarization decreases. On the one hand, changing our individual perspective is something we can each strive for. On the other hand, transforming systemic injustices, such as the gap between the rich and poor, cannot be accomplished through individual effort alone. Everyone in society must work together to effect this kind of change.

Happiness depends on both our attitude toward life – our ability to deal with issues as they arise – and our environment. For happiness to be sustainable, both the seed (the individual) and the field (the society) must be healthy. The individual and the society are the two wheels that pull the cart of happiness – both working together.

When Two Hunters Catch Three Rabbits

Why do humans live together when they fight so much over limited resources? Humans live together rather than alone because overall it is more beneficial for them. For example, when a man goes hunting alone, he may only catch one rabbit a day, but when two men go hunting together, they may catch three rabbits a day. Humans cooperate because pooling our skills and resources can be helpful to all of us.

However, cooperation doesn't yield good results every single time. It is often beneficial to cooperate when hunting, for example, but conflict may occur when trying to divide the kill. In fact, as the number of people among whom it must be divided increases, the potential for conflict also increases.

When many people get together and cooperate as a group, it is likely that each of them will profit more than if they worked alone. However, inevitably someone will draw the short straw and benefit less or perhaps not at all. When the number of people who suffer losses or do not benefit increases, so their anger and dissatisfaction may grow – this puts pressure on the system.

When an individual hunts and gathers food for themselves and their family group, this is pure self-sufficient production and consumption. The concept of distribution doesn't need to be considered. However, when two or more people work together, we must also consider distribution – it becomes as important as production.

So how should the three rabbits be shared between the two hunters? It is clear that each hunter should take one rabbit, but the question is how to divide the remaining extra rabbit that was caught thanks to the cooperation between the two hunters. The minimum number of rabbits each hunter can take is one while the maximum number is two. Taking three would mean one hunter was left with nothing to show for his hard work.

In this situation, wanting to take one rabbit cannot be considered greed since each person has the right to at least one rabbit. Wanting to take more than one but fewer than two is a want or desire. Wanting to take more than two rabbits, even all three, is greed. If you are greedy, you deprive others of their share, and sooner or later, you will suffer losses as well.

Individuals should refrain from being greedy, and social systems should regulate how far individuals are able to act on their greed. Also, social systems should ensure that a person's basic need (in this case receiving at least one rabbit) is fulfilled.

If social systems fail to either regulate the greed of their citizens or ensure their basic rights are provided for, everyone in society will eventually suffer. If one hunter takes all three rabbits, the other hunter won't have anything. The hunter who was ripped off is unlikely to cooperate with the first hunter the next time he is asked to help. The first hunter may have benefitted the most on this occasion by taking all three rabbits, but he won't be able to do the same thing again if the other hunter refuses to work with him anymore.

The two individuals need to agree on an adequate division of the extra rabbit. Ideally, each hunter should get one-and-a-half rabbits each, but realistic variables should also be considered. For example, during the day's hunt, if one hunter worked hard, but the other was lazy, the harder worker might feel dissatisfied about dividing their winnings equally. They might feel that the division should relate to the amount of effort each put in. But ideally each should receive half of what they have caught together.

Many of today's social problems stem from the combination of failure to ensure the basic rights of the disadvantaged and lack of regulation of the greed of the privileged. Consequently, there are many people whose survival is threatened and many who suffer from relative deprivation, while there is a small minority with much more than they could ever need.

Unfortunately, at a time when South Korea should have sought social consensus on distributive justice, neoliberalism swept the country. After the foreign currency crisis of 1998, Koreans came to believe that adopting neoliberalism was the only way they would be able to survive, so Korean society became highly competitive. The most prominent characteristic of neoliberalism is a winner-takes-all approach. A typical example is the concept that one smart person has the potential to make as much money as 100,000 average people. Encouraging competition in this way may increase productivity up to a certain degree, but there are limitations. A major problem with this is that, as income inequality intensifies, people who feel their hard work is not benefitting them as it should will naturally lose interest in working. As a result, society can begin to falter and lose its driving force.

If one person can catch one rabbit, and two people can catch three by cooperating and working cleverly, it is fair for each of them to get at least one but no more than two. The two hunters should reach an agreement that ensures each other's basic rights and, at the same time, minimizes relative deprivation.

If all the people in a community seek to fulfil their desire to have more than others, the community is sure to collapse. Ideally, each person should make an effort to contribute if they are able to, and everyone should get a fair share. However, since this may not always be realistic, it is necessary to adjust the distribution ratio according to each individual situation so that everyone has their needs taken care of.

Establish Yourself as a Good Example Before Criticizing Others

Most of us would like to be paid a good amount of money without necessarily having to work a lot. We would like to be promoted even if we don't really deserve it, or get accepted into good colleges even if we fall short of the academic qualifications. We wish to have a good seat even if we arrive late and everyone is already seated. And we would prefer everyone to overlook our mistakes. What if we learn to see these same situations from a different perspective? How would we feel if other people got salary increases while their workloads decreased, or were promoted while performing their jobs poorly, or were accepted into great colleges with mediocre grades? We would feel outraged at the unfairness of it all. We would resent these people, perhaps even blaming them for our own low earnings or for being passed over for the promotion we hoped for, or for our children being denied admission to their preferred college.

When we wish for a particular success, we usually don't think about the fact that our wish coming true often means a loss for someone else. Even if it crosses our mind, we shake it off, thinking, 'That's just the way life is.' We turn a blind eye to it, convincing ourselves that everything is okay. We tell ourselves, 'As long as I don't draw the short straw...'

At work, people are sometimes pressured to do something they are not comfortable with, maybe even unethical or immoral, either to keep their jobs when times are tight or to 'prove themselves' and get promoted. At other times, they may feel they need to climb the corporate ladder, using their colleagues as rungs to get where they want to go. Expressing how soul destroying it can be to be faced with such choices, someone once asked me the following question:

'The media occasionally reports on companies using slush funds to pay bribes. The company I work for is involved in these types of practices. Although I feel ashamed, I have no choice but to go along with it, as this is how the company operates. How should I handle this situation?'

You don't have to leave the company you work for just because the company's value system is different from yours. As long as the company doesn't ask you to leave, you can keep the job and do the right thing while you are working there. If you take the responsibility for deciding whether or not to quit, you can't help but hesitate. However, if you leave it up to the company to decide, you don't need to concern yourself with the decision. You become involved in conflicts when you criticize others; for example, when you say, 'What you're doing is wrong,' or 'This is poor practice.' In our lives, we will find problems wherever we look. Rather than simply criticizing others, it is important that we resolve not to act like those whose actions we consider morally problematic.

If you are determined not to engage in illegal or unethical behaviour, no matter how much you are paid, you can simply leave your job. However, if you're unable to do so and choose to act as others in the company do, you must understand that this is your choice and you must accept the consequences willingly.

You need to understand in advance the consequences that may follow. If you help your company defeat a competitor through unethical means, someday you may also be crushed in a similar way. Even if you are loyal to the company throughout this process, if your knowledge of illegal practice is exposed, you may still be personally liable for your actions. Understanding this possibility in advance is important, and you must be prepared to accept the consequences of your actions willingly rather than feeling wronged and resentful. In the long run, you will see that immediate rewards are a poor measure of success, especially if the route to achieving them is ethically or morally questionable.

If you wish to remain safe from potential repercussions, refrain from actions that you know might result in them. You will still be able to make a living, you may just have to find another role with a different company. I met a civil engineer who once claimed that his job required him to drink every day. He said that client hospitality was a big part of his role, and he had to 'wine and dine' clients in order to procure contracts. However, he quit drinking after participating in an 'Awakening Retreat'.* He later told me that he found he could still form good relationship

---

* A five-day retreat programme with the Jungto Society that guides people to experience changing their perspectives and begin their journey toward true happiness and freedom.

and secure contracts with his clients without drinking with them – it was a revelation!

When trying to improve something, we often say, 'Realistically, there isn't much I can do.' In most cases, this is a hasty generalization, not based on an actual attempt. Someone might say that it's impossible to do business with clients without drinking with them. However, of course it is possible. If you have no choice but to spend time in a drinking establishment with your clients, you can be there without drinking alcohol, or if pressured you can just pretend to drink. Also, you can do business with them without going to these events at all. At first, you might find yourself at a disadvantage and get fewer contracts. In the long run, though, if you're good at your job, you'll find a way to make it work. Clients might even come to appreciate your approach.

If your company encourages drinking and you try to avoid such occasions, your coworkers might complain, 'It's the company night out. Where do you think you're going?' or 'You're spoiling the fun.' However, you can make a ground rule right from the start. If you say, 'I will not drink alcohol,' and stick to it no matter what, people will eventually accept it. If you say, 'My dear colleagues, please excuse my absence,' and seek understanding from those around you, you can stay on friendly terms with them. Since you're choosing to go against the organization's culture in order to stick to your values, you may need to be apologetic. If you ride it out for about a year, things will sort themselves out.

On the other hand, if it is noted that you usually slip out of company social events or other 'extra-effort' situations for personal reasons, but you continue to compete for promotion opportunities, your coworkers may begin to resent you. To foster cordial relationships with them, the opposite approach is needed. You can tell your colleagues, 'You go first'. You can tell your boss you are happy for them to promote others before yourself by saying, 'I'll wait for the next opportunity. I'm still young.' If you adopt this attitude, you can head off potential conflicts in the workplace.

You may, of course, encounter resistance and criticism in the beginning. Some coworkers may tell you to quit or warn that you will be passed over for promotions. However, if you persist and continue to live according to your principles, the people around you will begin to accept this and may even start to change themselves. As time goes on, they will more fully accept and understand you. You just need to be consistent.

If we prioritize leading a happy life over money and social success, we have nothing to fear. We may need to put up with a certain amount of loss and criticism however, and this isn't easy, so if we lack clear and guiding life principles we may tend to give up.

When we're not centred, criticism bothers us. Of course we need to pay attention to what others say to us, but we don't have to be restricted by it or allow it to change our course of action. We concern ourselves with what others say because we don't want to receive criticism. Since we don't want to be criticized, we always try to be nice to others.

You're born into this world and spend your life competing fiercely for a small gain. Let's say, one day, you find out that you are terminally ill, or you suddenly get fired from the company you've been devoted to for your whole working life. Imagine how angry and resentful you would feel. You may ask yourself, 'What have I lived for?' You may feel that you've lived in vain. Therefore, competing so fiercely is definitely not a good way to live.

If you truly believe that bribery is unethical, you should refuse to engage in it. If you find that work-related drinks gatherings aren't beneficial to your health, avoid them tactfully. At the same time, be the first to volunteer for unpleasant tasks, such as difficult meetings or cleaning, and stop hankering after promotions. Maintain your principles while conceding secondary issues and willingly engaging with tasks that others may be reluctant to take on. In this way, your coworkers are more likely to support you than resent you.

When you want to overcome the contradictory realities in life and take the path that allows everyone to be happy, resolve to be the one who will take the first step. If you become an example first, instead of criticizing others, you will find abundant hope and happiness in life.

How to Be Happy and Benefit Others at the Same Time

Happiness that is obtained at someone else's expense cannot last long. What, then, is true happiness? Is there a way for us to all be happy together?

These questions plagued the Buddha 2,600 years ago, before he left his family home in search of truth. He realized the inadequacy of a life that was based on acquiring material objects. He discovered the truth that, as long as our primary goal is to possess more and more, we can never achieve happiness together.

Everyone wants to be happy. However, in the long run, happiness based on selfish desires will lead to unhappiness and even outright misery. From this moment forward, we need to live lives that benefit others as well as ourselves. If you do things that benefit you while at the same time creating disadvantages for others, people will not tolerate this indefinitely. On the other hand, if you are living in such a way as to benefit others but it requires you to sacrifice, you will not be happy in that situation. Happiness is only sustainable when both parties are able to benefit. Therefore, we need to work together to build a society where people enjoy mutual benefits.

We need wisdom and courage to live a life that is positive for us as well as good for others. For example, keeping a positive mindset at work is ideal. However, if you witness injustice at your workplace, you also need to be able to say, 'Hey, this isn't right.' You need to be principled, a person quietly leading by example, whether that means standing up for what is right, helping others, or volunteering to perform difficult or unpopular tasks.

An office worker once asked me a question about how to deal with discrimination against temporary employees at the workplace: 'There are 30 people on my team. Only five are permanent employees, and the rest are temporary contract workers. Temporary employees are subject to discrimination in terms of pay and benefits compared to those with permanent positions. I don't feel comfortable working with the temporary workers, and I feel bad for them. Some of them may be forced to leave the company when it's time for contract renewal. My heart feels heavy because I'm the one who will have to terminate their contracts.'

If you're not planning to quit your job, it is not right to turn away from the task you're assigned to do, even if you don't feel happy about it. It's understandable that you don't feel comfortable about working with people who are discriminated against when they do the same amount of work as everybody else. However, this is how things sometimes operate in the current system, and one person can't change everything all at once. In any case, if this is a task that has been assigned to you, the best you can do is to explain the company policy clearly to these temporary workers and be as fair as possible with them during the contract termination process. When some of the laid-off workers inevitably resent you, instead of ignoring them or trying to shut them down, lend them a sympathetic ear.

Your energy would be put to better use working out ways to lay off fewer people rather than dreading and worrying about something that will not happen for several months. It would be better for you to spend your time either improving the efficiency of your team or proposing creative ideas to increase the amount of work your team has to deal with.

We live in an unjust world. However, we need to try to make circumstances as fair as possible. This is progress. At the same time, we also need to acknowledge the inequality that exists as part of our current reality. If we insist on equality without acknowledging the inequality that exists already in the world, the change we are hoping to see becomes nothing more than a distant dream. Then, we won't be able to adjust in the real world. Conversely, if we accept the current inequality and settle without making any effort to encourage equality in the future, we won't be able to make real progress.

We must plant our feet firmly in the current unjust reality, but work towards our goal of improving things and moving towards a fairer and more equal world. Then, we'll find ourselves moving away from an unequal reality toward an equitable world one step at a time. When we take on this perspective, we can maintain our vision but also be realistic at the same time. In this way, we will be able to make our dreams come true in real life.

Realizing your dreams within reality means first acknowledging and accepting your current conditions and then investigating ways to ensure that temporary workers are no longer discriminated against in your company.

For example, in the past, there used to be a significant wage gap between men and women. Rather than continuing to accept this, as society started to change people made persistent efforts to narrow the gap, and some improvements have been made. Likewise, if you see problems in the different ways permanent workers and temporary workers are treated at your company, you should not turn a blind eye. Instead of avoiding the temporary workers or being disappointed that you're not able to resolve this problem immediately, you should continue to investigate and look for potential solutions that might improve the situation.

Leading a happy life should be your priority no matter what anyone else says. Your efforts for social change will have a ripple effect when you yourself are happy. If you have a positive attitude, a smile on your face, and get along well with others, you will receive a lot of support as you talk about your ideas and work towards ways of making the world better.

However, even if we make efforts to make the world a better place we must not expect to see immediate results. When we begin any project, we hope to see quick outcomes to assure us we are doing well, but the world doesn't work that way. Our efforts sometimes bear fruit, but other times, they don't. And sometimes things take longer than we expect. If our efforts are successful, that's great, but if they are not, we can always go back to the drawing board and try again. If we fail despite our best efforts, then we must try something else.

One thing you should keep in mind is that whatever you do, instead of doing it solely for the benefit of society and/or for other people, you should do it because it's rewarding and fun for you. Then, you will be happy regardless of the outcome. If you succeed, you'll feel happy that you were successful. But if you don't, you will still feel happy because you had fun and maybe even learned something in the process.

Many people think that if they don't succeed, it means they've failed, but that's not exactly true. There is no such thing as failure. If I start building something and lay the foundation before I die, my successors or descendants can build on it. If they are also unable to finish it, others can continue the work.

Change takes time. If the goal is to bring about significant, fundamental change, it may take a very long time. But if you set an easy goal, it can be achieved much more quickly.

Determination to see something through to completion because you are the one who started it, or it was your idea in the first place, is an urge that stems from greed. Likewise, putting in less effort or even disregarding something because you're not the one who initiated it may also originate from greed.

Avoid being overly proud of doing good deeds or imbuing too much meaning into them. Don't take yourself too seriously, and you'll be happy whatever the outcome.

The world thinks caring for others is unquestionably good and calls it 'altruistic'. But people often fall into the trap of wanting to be congratulated or compensated for their selflessness. If you think that you are making an effort for others, be sure that you are not expecting to be rewarded in some way for your actions – if you are, this will lead to resentment.

Rather than congratulating ourselves on the sacrifices we make for others, it is preferable to understand that helping others is actually a route to helping ourselves. This concept can be expressed with the

Buddhist term *Jari-ita*, which means that benefiting oneself is the same as benefiting others.

Plants provide bees with nectar through flowers, while bees help plants bear fruit by transferring pollen. In the same way, we must live a life that is good for us, as well as benefitting others. When we all come to understand that helping others also benefits us as individuals we will stop regarding those acts as sacrifices. Then we will truly be on the path to shared happiness.

Part 05

Practice Being Happier Today Than Yesterday

As we travel through our lives, all kinds of events occur. Loved ones die, financial pressures strike. You may even experience betrayal at the hands of a person you once cared deeply for. Nothing occurs without reason. However, these events don't happen because they are God's will or because you committed sins in your past life. They are not mere coincidences either. You just don't know the reason behind them.

It is the same with the weather. There are times when hail suddenly falls during the summer, when a pocket of warm, spring-like weather appears for a moment in the winter, and when it's cool like autumn during the summer. However, on average, summer is warmer, and winter is colder. Similarly, if you have a pure heart and live with good intentions, there is a higher chance of good things happening to you. On the other hand, if you have an impure heart and live with malicious intentions, there is a higher chance of bad things happening to you.

When problems occur, acknowledging and accepting what has already happened is the first step toward finding a solution. One should willingly accept the consequences of one's actions. But if you don't want to face such consequences again, you should be mindful of never repeating the same actions. Discover the exact cause of those consequences and eliminate them. If we seek solutions by paying close attention to what causes the issues in our lives, instead of constantly running away from our problems, the process becomes a challenge instead of an ordeal.

Letting Go of Judgements

We often see the world through a binary lens. We think to ourselves, 'This is right; that is wrong,' or 'I am right; you are wrong.' That's why we're continually trapped by our own judgements and tripped up by our own expectations.

Imagine a garden of flowers with all sorts of beautiful blossoms. They do not argue with one other or compete with one other to be crowned the most beautiful. Imagine, however, that when you are looking at the garden, you think, 'This rose is beautiful but why is that tulip so ugly?' The thought would not stop there but would continue as an endless stream. You might think, 'Maybe those who did good deeds in their previous lives became roses, and those who did bad things became tulips.'

These kinds of beliefs are sometimes referred to as 'past lives', 'astrological signs', or 'punishment from heaven', depending on your worldview. A rose is just a rose; a tulip is just a tulip. There is no hidden meaning, and neither is better nor worse than the other.

In our world, some people like roses, others like tulips, and some prefer azaleas. People's tastes and preferences vary extensively. There is no way to sort good preferences from bad ones, or to rank them from better to worse. When you approach people's differences with an attitude of curiosity and discovery, conflicts and arguments simply do not arise.

I was invited to give a talk at Google in 2014, where a staff member asked: 'This year has been especially complicated and hard to swallow. From the conflicts in the Middle East to the Ebola virus outbreak, it feels as if the whole universe is drawing to a close. What's really going on?'

These kinds of events have happened all through human history, and they will no doubt continue to happen. The world is not so complex. The world only seems complicated when we lack the capacity to understand the changes that are happening.

The solution to wars and conflicts is not so complicated. It can often be found by addressing the greed and inequalities which are often at the source of anger and violent actions. Violent suppression of protest or retaliatory action is effective only in the short term.

Aggressors may appear placated or defeated, but they inevitably resume and conflicts escalate again. That's why we need a different method of dealing with them. Responding with violent force does not solve such problems. A different kind of response is needed.

The first step is understanding human psychology. No matter how ridiculous the claims of one side or another may sound, it is important to explore why each feels compelled to behave as they do. When we react emotionally, saying 'An eye for an eye, and a tooth for a tooth,' and responding with violence of our own, the situation only deteriorates.

Requiring subjugation or contrition before agreeing to negotiate is not the right attitude either. Authentic dialogue requires a willingness to sit at the table without attaching conditions or expectations. The time to ask for an apology is after the dialogue. Requiring an apology beforehand undermines the willingness to talk.

For dialogue to work, the stronger party needs to take the first steps toward making concessions. Even when dealing with gangs and terrorists, approaching the situation gently is more effective than declaring war. When the more powerful side makes a concession, it is often praised and they are congratulated for taking a step in the right direction. However, when the weaker party makes a concession, it is often referred to as submission or capitulation, something they were forced to do. They will feel humiliated, and this will motivate them to resist further. In order to resolve conflicts, the side with more power needs to begin to make concessions.

If we could view from a broader perspective, we would come to realize that the seeds of such tragedies are sown long before the disputes and violence actually erupt. That is why simply punishing one side or another leaves the root causes of the conflict unresolved. True peace requires understanding and acceptance of the unique and intrinsic qualities of the people and their struggles on each side. When we accept reality and build systems that promote positive changes, we can resolve conflicts, making the world more harmonious. Judgements about past actions – about whether or not they conform to our moral standards – are for another day.

Much of the anger in the world arises because this order is reversed. We usually don't start by seeking to understand the reality of the situation, but instead, we jump immediately to judgements about right and wrong based on our own standards. This process leads to arguments, aggression, anger and further misunderstanding.

The same applies to individuals. Imagine that, while riding on a crowded bus, someone suddenly pushes you. At first, you would be shocked, then you would become angry and feel wronged. If you later found out that you had stepped on that person's foot and broken their toe, you might feel differently. Then, even though you were pushed, you would say, 'Oh no, I'm very sorry.' However, if you never realized that you had stepped on their toe, you would protest angrily, saying, 'Why did you shove me?' Then, that person would also get angrier, and the conflict would escalate.

There's a wiser way to deal with this type of situation. Before judging, look inside yourself and ask whether your own actions may have contributed to the situation. You should examine whether rejecting the other person based on your insistence on being right may have hurt that person and brought you trouble. Looking for the cause within yourself will help you solve both individual and social problems, while blaming others will not. Even if you don't discover the root cause, refraining from emotional confrontation prevents the situation from becoming worse. It won't be easy, but you need to make a rational choice, unhindered by emotions. This is not to say that you should blame yourself or that you should silently tolerate unfair or aggressive treatment. Just don't let emotions carry you away and blind you from the essence of the problem.

Trying to get even after you think you have been treated unfairly solves nothing. Acting as if someone is your enemy only results in turning that person into an actual enemy, and violence just begets more violence. Unfair treatment should be disclosed with the goal of preventing others having to endure similar treatment. This requires detachment from our own judgements. When disclosing a problem, it must be done thoroughly and persistently, free from the sway of pressure and temptations. To do this, you need both courage and wisdom.

When discussions about unfairness are cloaked in anger, your statements are reduced to the level of personal vengeance. As a result, this evolves into a lonely and painful battle in which others can't help you. If, detached from hatred and resentment, you manage to act calmly with the aim of resolving the problem for yourself as well as for posterity, you will find that people will empathize with you and support you. Then, this process will both heal your own pain and bring about changes that will benefit the world.

Insightfulness, the Wisdom of Seeing the Whole

When we look at something, we typically see it from just one angle. It could be from our own perspective as individuals, as parents, or from the perspective of a group we are part of. However, although we are viewing from this fixed perspective, we mistakenly think we understand the entire issue. We mistake our biases for our convictions.

During a Dharma talk, someone might nod their head and say, 'Yes, Sunim, that's right.' Should I assume that means they understood what I said? Someone else might shake their head and say, 'No, that's not true.' Does that mean that they didn't understand? No, that's not what it means. It only signifies that the person who nods their head shares the same opinion as the one I have expressed, while the person who shakes their head has a different opinion from mine.

We look at the world through distorted lenses, shaped and coloured by our own experiences, biases, and capacity for understanding. Through these lenses, we often judge what we see as right or wrong. It is as if we are wearing different coloured glasses, thinking that whatever we see is really yellow, red or blue. We're like blind men touching different parts of an elephant. One touches the leg and says that the elephant is like a pillar; another touches the trunk and compares the elephant to a snake. Each mistakes a part for the whole.

In the same way, we view the world based on our limited experience of our immediate surroundings and our own perspectives, and we say, 'This is the truth,' or 'This is correct.' In using only our own framework to try and understand everything, we don't see our children, parents, or spouses as they really are. When we are looking at our home, we don't see our neighbours' homes. When we focus on our own country, we don't see other people's countries. When we are considering our religion, we can't understand other people's religions. We're continually clinging to our own points of view while insisting that we are right.

When people ask me questions, it might seem like I'm providing answers, but that's not what is really happening. I'm simply helping them to see situations from different angles. When someone approaches the situation from the front, I ask, 'What does it look like from the back?' When somebody is looking at one side, I ask, 'What's it like around the other side?' If they view it from the top, I ask, 'What's going on at the bottom?' It is important to learn how to see the totality. Considering an issue from just one fixed and particular angle is bias; seeing the whole is insightfulness or wisdom.

When we let go of attachments based on one-sided perspectives, we see that what we previously thought of as problems aren't really problems after all. When we attain the wisdom to really see and consider the whole, many of our troubles simply disappear, just as the darkness in a dark room dissipates once the light is turned on.

To awaken is to open both eyes and see the whole, instead of only considering one side or allowing your biases to direct your viewpoint. Awakening means overcoming prejudices and judgements that are based on a one-sided perception. To awaken is to see multiple perspectives simultaneously: to see others along with ourselves, others' homes as well as our own homes, others' religions at the same time as our own, others' countries as well as our own, the North along with the South. By looking at the whole, you can see the truth and you can follow the right path.

A young man once spoke to me, saying that the world we live in seems very unfair. He asked me the following question: 'Why am I only 170cm (5ft 7in) tall and so unattractive? Many men are over 183cm (6ft) and handsome. And why are there people in the world who are wealthy while others are poor? Why are there people who are happy while others are unhappy? Is this the law of nature? Is this the world that God and the Buddha spoke about?'

Why do we think that the conditions we live in are unfair? If you have been born a woman into this world where men are privileged over women, you may lament, 'I wish I hadn't been born a woman!' However, there is nothing inherently good or bad about being born either a man or a woman. It is just that you live in a society that gives privileges to some that are not granted to others. If a woman laments, 'I wish I hadn't been born a woman!' it's only because she doesn't have the same privileges as a man. If the custom of granting privileges based on gender were to disappear, this issue wouldn't arise. Therefore, the social discrimination women face is the real problem; being born a woman is neither inherently bad nor unfair.

Saying that those who were good in a past life are born into wealth is just a way for the privileged to rationalize their wealth.

In addressing problems people face in life, many false teachings have been propagated as part of religion. These range from, 'It is a punishment for not believing in God,' to 'These problems are a punishment for sins committed in previous lives.' Both Jesus and the Buddha actually instructed their followers not to discriminate against people of different genders, different skin colours, or different abilities.

Our present society tends to view tall people as more attractive and short people as less attractive and somewhat inferior. However, every height has both advantages and disadvantages. Some situations are advantageous for tall people; others are advantageous for short people. When one person is tall, and another person is short, the truth of the matter is that they have different heights. On the other hand, whether height causes attractiveness or unattractiveness is a cultural issue, and a matter of personal preference on the part of the person making that judgement. It has no basis in objective reality.

An elephant was not born big because of good deeds in its previous life; a mouse isn't small because of sins committed in its past life. There is no inequality in nature. Just because snakes eat frogs, it doesn't mean that a snake was born superior to a frog. They're just different species, doing what they do.

Over the course of history, discrimination between the nobility and commoners has disappeared in Korea. That's why people no longer lament, 'Why was I born a commoner?' Things are different now.

In the same way, we need to update the way we think about height, remembering that small, tall and everything in between is beautiful. Why on earth is being short a problem? From an environmental standpoint, being short actually has many advantages – less material for clothing, smaller beds and smaller people generally consume less food. Because they consume less, being smaller may be said to contribute to conserving resources and energy.

We need to consider whether or not our beliefs are accurate reflections of reality. Looking at something through the lens of our prejudices is like trying to find something by groping around in a dark room. Maybe we'll find it, and maybe we won't. We might bump into something and hurt ourselves. We may fall. We might mistakenly grab hold of something else. However, when we turn on the light and see the entire room, we are much more likely to find what we are looking for right away.

When we gain insight, we can see everything in the world as it really is. Then, the frantic mind, trying to decide whether something is right or wrong, or whether to do this or that, is stilled and becomes quiet. Your heart becomes lighter. The darkness inside your mind instantly gives way to light.

We need to cultivate the wisdom to see the whole instead of clinging to society's (and our own) stereotypes and fixed notions. Then we can live, not as slaves to our circumstances, but as masters of our own lives.

The Merit of Comforting Others

In August 1996, the barrier that divided South Korea and North Korea in my heart fell thanks to an incident that occurred while I was taking an historical tour in China. Our young Korean-Chinese guide asked me for help, saying, 'North Korean children are starving to death.' He pleaded with me several times, but I didn't believe him because I thought it was nonsense.

He insisted, 'It's true. Go and see it for yourself.' So I boarded a boat on the Amnokgang River, still thinking that this couldn't be true. However, on the North Korean side of the river, I saw emaciated children sitting on the ground, weak and listless. I was shocked and called out to them, but they didn't raise their heads. Usually, hungry children will follow strangers around to try and obtain anything they can get, even just a piece of candy, so it was strange that these kids were so unresponsive. The young guide explained that North

Korean children will never beg from outsiders even though they are hungry because they are taught from a very young age that to do so is to disgrace their country. So, I tried to throw the food I had with me towards them on the riverbank. However, the guide stopped me, saying, 'You can't do that because we are at the China-North Korea border.'

My heart ached. Even birds fly across the river to find food on the other side. So I was appalled that I couldn't hand food over to people who were dying of starvation just because we were divided by a border.

I became painfully aware of the harsh reality of a divided nation. I couldn't help the starving children of my own Korean kin, who were only a few metres away, but I could travel abroad to help children of faraway nations like India and the Philippines.

From that point on, the wall that divided the two Koreas has vanished from my heart. Since that day, I have not been able to stop helping the North Korean people, no matter how much suspicion and criticism are pointed my way.

I adhere to three principles when helping people who are in need: The hungry should have food; the sick should be treated; children should be educated.

Such principles are reflected in the last words of the Buddha. When Ananda asked the Buddha, 'After you pass away, to whom should we make our offerings to accumulate merit?' The Buddha said, 'There are four types of offerings that are as honourable as the offerings made to me. First is to feed the hungry, second is to treat the sick, third is to help and comfort the poor and lonely, and fourth is to protect the pure-minded practitioners.'

Currently, on Earth, there is a huge number of people starving to death or suffering from severe malnutrition. Among the nearly eight billion people around the world today, almost 10 per cent are estimated to be enduring extreme poverty and living on less than the equivalent of USD $1.90 a day. Many suffer from severe malnutrition and cannot dream of receiving adequate medical care, let alone sending their children to school. Diseases that are easily treatable, such as paratyphoid fever and tuberculosis, cost relatively little to treat in South Korea, but the extremely poor in some other parts of the world simply don't have access to such treatment. Therefore, if they contract the disease, they have no choice but to await death. Almost 10 per cent of people in the world suffer from such extreme poverty.

Between 1995 and 1998, about three million people died of hunger and disease in North Korea. The death of this many people means that those who survived also suffered greatly as their family members, friends and neighbours died.

When we hear about those who are suffering, we generally respond in one of two ways. One is avoidance; people who respond this way are those who can't understand the suffering of others if they have not experienced it themselves. The other group consists of those who become distressed and consumed by worry. Empathizing with other people's suffering may seem better than ignoring it, but the people who respond in either of these two ways are basically the same because they are caught up in their own thoughts and reactions. Neither response is partciularly helpful to those suffering.

After I saw the starving North Korean children, I cried. They were famished and looked so desolate. It would be difficult to explain to anyone who hadn't seen such a terrible sight for themselves.

When you're participating in humanitarian relief work, you sometimes feel angry because of people's indifference, and sometimes you become deeply saddened because you feel powerless. However, being sad doesn't help the suffering people in any way and doesn't change anything. It only makes your own heart ache.

Therefore, instead of falling into distress when you see people suffering, you should look for ways to help, even if you are only able to help one person, and you should be thankful that you are still healthy and able to earn a living. Rather than worrying all night about the people who are suffering, and wallowing in your own sadness, it is better to get a good night's sleep and rise again the next day determined to explore options that might actually help.

When I ask others to help the needy, I often hear the following kinds of responses: 'It's hard enough for me to make a living. How can I possibly help others?' 'There are so many poor people in South Korea. Shouldn't we help them first?' 'Would my small donation make any difference at all, really?'

When there are ten people who need help, but you can only help one, you'll feel powerless. However, you just need to do what you can with what you have even if you are only able to help one or two people.

Do you think there are only ten people who need help in this world? Of course not. Counting the number of people who need help and lamenting your inability to assist them all will only make you miserable. If you can help one person, go ahead. And if you're able to help two, you can do that. Just do what you can.

It's good to aspire to gain the ability to help more people. If you set an aspirational goal that is not rooted in greed or ego, you will build your capacity to help ten people even if you can only help one person now. If you set a more ambitious aspiration, you may find you are able to help a hundred people by finding creative new ways to make it possible. Your sincere dedication will move the hearts of the people around you, and then unexpected miracles can occur.

When we set out to help others, we are rewarded many times over with the satisfaction we feel in goals accomplished. However, many people think that they will be happy when they receive something from others. This is because we have been brainwashed to think that way by the culture we live in.

If you live with the belief that happiness comes from receiving, you'll continue to seek external blessings and always be hungry for more, even if you become economically affluent and actually have enough. Then, you won't be able to stop feeling poor all your life. If you're lucky, you may enjoy temporary happiness, but it won't last.

For example, let's suppose that a friend of yours gives you $1,000 every month. Would happiness be the only thing you would feel? How would you feel whenever you meet that friend to receive the money? You might feel beholden to them and take care not to offend them. It would be difficult to refuse anything they might ask you to do in return, regardless of whether it was beyond your abilities or morally wrong.

Those who like receiving help depend on others. With time, as these people become financially stable, they often don't want to keep in touch with those who helped them when they were struggling. This is because they don't want their past to be revealed, and they would prefer to forget about the help they received and instead believe that they did it all on their own.

If you want to realize your wish of receiving things from others, you need to be in a position that attracts and justifies the help of others, such as being ill, poor, miserable, or having some kind of misfortune befall you. Sometimes, those who like to receive help make themselves deliberately pitiful. This is not limited to material things. Those who want to receive things, whatever they may be, will always feel that whatever they receive is not enough, no matter how much they are given. They feel happy only temporarily when they receive something, but the happiness won't last long.

On the other hand, if you give and share, you'll feel rich regardless of how much you possess. You don't have to give something big. You can just give whatever you're able to share.

Giving food to a hungry person, giving clothes to a person who needs them, and helping a child that has fallen down get back up are all acts of giving. As you continue giving, you'll find out that you end up benefiting much more than you would by keeping what you gave.

We all suffer from various difficulties in life. However, when we look around, there are many people who live each day in distress without the most basic necessities. When we understand their pain and try to comfort and help them, our problems seem to become smaller and lighter. We realize, 'My problems are nothing at all compared to theirs. I am a happy person with many blessings after all.'

When you help others, you transform from a person who used to dwell on trivial things and suffered as a result into someone who feels grateful and happy. This is the merit of helping others.

Different Levels of Love

Every January, I lead a pilgrimage to India, retracing the footsteps of the Buddha. On the pilgrimage, we always encounter children begging. They stretch out their dirty hands, saying 'Baksheesh, baksheesh.' Soft-hearted Korean pilgrims take pity on them, rummage through their pockets, and hand each child a coin.

Somehow, as time passes, those who felt sorry for the children and willingly gave them coins at first start to feel annoyed. It's because the children come back to get more instead of leaving after receiving one. 'I gave you a coin already,' they say. 'Don't give it to him. He had one from me just now.'

They fuss like this. The coin they give is worth about ten cents. After giving one coin, they become cross if the children try to get more than one. This is our level of helping others. We make up our minds to help others, but it's not easy to maintain this mindset regardless of our circumstances and conditions. For this to be possible, we must have, in Christian terms, the love of Jesus in our hearts. In Buddhist terms, we need the heart of a bodhisattva.

Kshitigarbha is a bodhisattva who goes down to hell to endlessly save all sentient beings. Even if someone he has previously saved returns to hell, Kshitigarbha never gives up and saves them again.

It would be difficult enough to save someone who is in hell. If that same person returns to hell two or three times after making the same mistakes, most of us would say to ourselves, 'I already saved them, I don't need to save them again!' After saving someone who is in hell, if we saw that person there again, we'd likely give up on the idea of saving them for the second time. This is our level of compassion. Kshitigarbha's compassion, on the other hand, is boundless. He maintains his vow to save all sentient beings and continues saving them no matter how many times they fall back into hell.

I began to help the Dalits (people belonging to the lowest caste) in India after an experience I had during my first pilgrimage there in 1991. On my first night in Calcutta, I went out to buy some water, and I encountered a young woman begging with a baby in her arms. The moment she saw me, she grabbed my garment and led me to a small store, where she pointed to a can of baby formula that she wanted me to buy for her. I asked the shopkeeper for the price. It was 60 rupees.

At that moment I remembered some advice I had received before traveling to India. I'd been advised not to give more than one rupee to any begging child since one rupee was a substantial amount in India. Based on this advice, 60 rupees sounded like a lot of money. I was startled by the price, so I left the shop without buying the baby formula for the young woman.

After buying the two bottles of water I needed, I returned to the hotel, where I asked my travel guide how much 60 rupees was worth in Korean won. He said that it was about 2,400 KRW, or about $2 USD at that time. This made me feel terrible.

The woman had asked me to buy her a can of baby formula that cost only $2, and I reacted as though she had asked me to hand over all of my possessions.

I had participated in various social movements and urged people to help the poor. At Buddhist temples, I talked to people about the need to alleviate human suffering, and yet I had turned away from real suffering that was happening right in front of my own eyes. I was utterly shocked by my own contradictory behaviour.

After this shocking realization, I gave away my extra clothes and most of the money that I had with me. Subsequently, many more children began following me around, and my fellow travellers complained a great deal.

Days later, we came upon a village in the countryside, where I saw a small group of children sitting together. I called out to offer them some candy, but instead of coming to take the candy they ran away. Once again, I was shocked. In my encounter with the young woman begging to buy formula for her baby, the problem was that I had refused to help. After the episode with the children who refused my offer of candy, I realized that the children begged because travellers kept giving them things, not because of their poverty. The children in the countryside were just as poor, but because nobody ever gave them anything, they didn't beg. When I tried to give them candy, the children became shy and ran away. I concluded that it was the travellers who caused the children to beg. Realizing that giving was not necessarily always good, I decided not to give anything more to any begging children.

Later, on my way to the Sujata Temple near Bodh Gaya, I passed a young boy begging on the street; he had no legs. When I refused, he followed me, dragging himself with his hands for more than 1km (¾ mile).

I began to question whether I was doing the right thing in not giving anything to a child who had made such an effort to get to me. I began to doubt myself. Once again, my perspective changed.

I concluded that the real issue wasn't the children's attitudes, it was mine. I started to reflect on how I could help children without turning them into, or perpetuating their role as, beggars. I eventually built a school, a hospital and water wells for the Dalits in Dungeshwari, India. Thanks to my mistakes and my efforts to correct them, I finally gained an opportunity to do something truly good.

Had I simply been generous from the start, I would never have thought of building a school in India. This is why making mistakes isn't necessarily a bad thing. When we recognize our mistakes, repent, and learn from them, there is a greater chance that we may end up developing true love and compassion for others.

Happiness Lies in Fun and Rewarding Activities

Today, South Korea is better off economically, and we're more open-minded than before, but we haven't changed much in the sense that we are still tied down to something. In the past, people were trapped by class or to land as slaves or serfs. Now, we're enslaved by our need for money in a capitalist society. Whether we are ensnared by class, land or money, it's all the same – something stands in between us and our freedom.

There are two types of situation in which people feel happy. We feel happy when we're doing something we want to do and we feel happy when we are contributing in some way to the wellbeing and welfare of others. However, if we only pursue what feels good in the present, we may come to regret this or feel empty about it later on. On the other hand, if we focus too much on potential future benefits, we may experience hardship in our present lives and become weary

– always heading towards something we never quite reach. The best choice is to balance the two options and enjoy things in the present that will also benefit us in the future. We should benefit others as well as ourselves. To make this possible, there shouldn't be a gap between activities we enjoy and activities that are beneficial to others. If we consider helping others part of our job and we also have fun while working, we won't need to add in an extra activity after work to relieve stress.

There are many ways we can live our lives. In my case, I try to donate my time, energy and resources to places where they can be most beneficial. For example, there is little you can buy with 1,000 KRW or $1 USD in Korea. Yet the same amount of money can feed five children in India. That dollar is worth a lot more in India than in South Korea or the USA, so it is more rewarding to spend the same amount of money to help the people in India. Essentially, I seek out locations with the most suffering and hardship, because in those places I can assist a greater number of people and it feels much more gratifying as well.

People generally want to go to heaven or paradise after they die, but I do not share that desire. They say heaven is a good place, which means I wouldn't have much to do there. On the other hand, if I go to hell, I'll have plenty of work to do. Since my limited abilities will be more useful there, I'm sure I would find it more fun and rewarding. Therefore, when Christians spreading the gospel on the street tell me, 'If you don't believe in Jesus, you'll go to hell,' I simply say, 'Thank you.'

No matter who you are, you have unique talents and abilities that enable you to do things both that you like to do and that you can do well. Just ask yourself where your talents are most needed and where they can be most effective. Working in a way that uses your abilities effectively makes the experience more enjoyable and rewarding, enabling you to become more self-confident. Negative thoughts about your life and your path, questioning your worth and your abilities, will not occur to you. When you approach life with an attitude focused on how you can better help others, you will be much more energized.

Using your talents in an effective manner also relates to choosing a job. Making a living can be hard, and career options can be quite limited. Just finding a job with a good salary may be considered a success in itself. If you then succeed in snagging a better position, you would also be expected to fulfill higher expectations, resulting in a heavy workload. Also, your spending will increase because you had to meet the increased demands of your role, as well as expectations of your family and friends. Consequently, even if your job is tough and you hate having to do it, you cannot afford to quit, so you find yourself leading an exhausting life. However, you don't have to continue living that way.

As long as you are confident you can earn enough to live on, it is wiser for you to choose work that you will find both fun and rewarding. Let go of your desire to work for a particularly prestigious corporation and your focus on achieving for status and a high income. Instead, seek to become a person who is of real value; you will grow happy and make a positive impact on the world.

I don't accept compensation for my Dharma talks. If I was paid, it would be labour, but since I am not, it is voluntary work. When people are forced to work without compensation, we call it 'exploitation' or 'enslavement'. When people are paid adequately for their work, we call it 'labour'. Similarly, if people are promised $100 in return for a certain amount of work but are only paid $50, this is considered unethical. However, if people don't expect compensation for their work but happily contribute their efforts for the good of the world, we call it volunteering. Therefore, when you choose a job you are happy with because you feel the work is of value, despite low pay and a high workload, this is similar to volunteering.

On the other hand, if you have a job with a high salary but a light workload, you are living an indebted life. In this respect, volunteer work, making use of our abilities to the fullest without pay, is the most advanced form of labour and the path to true freedom.

In the future, the world will place higher value on those who choose jobs based on their interest or how best they can contribute to the world, rather than how much money they can earn. These are happy people who shine wherever they are, whatever they do. In this sense, the significant increase in the number of people donating their talents and volunteering is a positive phenomenon.

When you become aware of places that need you, places where you can be highly useful, you will gain confidence and discover the true value in your life. True happiness begins when you are freed from obsessing about money. Instead of focusing on how much money you can possibly make, you should base your decisions on deciding where your efforts will be the most valuable. It is worthwhile to realize your dreams and ideals even if you have to spend your own money to do so. After all, true happiness lies in doing something fun and rewarding.

How to Organize Your Time to Live Happily

Once, a woman asked me how she could attain self-actualization, saying that she felt apathetic: 'I've held jobs and had various experiences, but I have never been able to feel satisfied. Since my children began going to school, I have more free time, but I'm not happy, and I keep wondering why not. It occurred to me that I've lived without a dream for some time. What do I need to do to discover what my dream might be?'

Having a job outside the home and earning money is not the only way to attain self-actualization. If your partner is making enough money to support your family, you don't need to earn extra just to buy expensive clothes or live in a bigger house. Instead, you can volunteer at places like churches, temples, or charity organizations, doing things like admin, cooking, cleaning, or serving the needy. Then, your spirit may improve, and you will enjoy new energy and vigour.

If you do this, you will acquire a broader world view and will be less likely to be bothered by trivial things. You might find you are more tolerant and understanding towards your partner and children. When you aren't doing anything worthwhile with your life, you may be easily dominated by the smallest desires and annoyances.

When you use your free time to volunteer, while taking care of your family, you'll feel grateful to your partner as their income enables you to do this. As a result, when you return from a day of volunteering, for example, you're likely to be more careful and attentive to your family.

You have no obligation to feel inferior to your partner because they are earning an income and you are not. When you volunteer as much as your schedule permits, that will enable you to attain self-actualization. On the other hand, forcing yourself into a job just to make some extra money is akin to enslaving yourself for money.

There are three things you can do to take your first steps on the path toward self-actualization. The first is donating money to the poor. The second is expressing gratitude during prayer instead of requesting good fortune. The third is doing volunteer work in gratitude for the blessings you have already received. Then, you will naturally attain the self-actualization you are seeking.

Once you have been volunteering for about three years, you will find you become much happier and more emotionally stable. Then, you can seek employment if that's what you want. After you have worked hard as a volunteer without any pay, you'll be happy and at ease no matter what kind of job you take subsequently. If, instead of taking my advice, you are determined to get a job under the belief that you can self-actualize only by having an enviable career, you will be constantly under pressure, perpetuating your suffering.

When I say that you should volunteer and contribute to society, this doesn't mean that you should go to extremes, abandoning your marriage and giving away all your money to join a monastic order. You don't need to participate in extreme political or social movements at the risk of going to jail. What I mean is that, if you have 100 units of time, you can spend 80 of them on your own affairs and spend the remaining 20 units on addressing global issues and helping others, working for social change. That way, you can lead your own life that includes family, hobbies, jobs and marriage, as well as volunteering.

If you spend 20 per cent of your available time volunteering, your life will become significantly better. When you do something rewarding, it invigorates your life, making you more productive during the remaining 80 per cent. Then, no matter what you're doing, you'll be able to lead a happy life.

What does it mean to set aside part of your time and make good use of it? At Google, they have what they call the 20 per cent project. Based on this system, employees are able to freely use 20 per cent of their work time on whatever they are interested in. Surprisingly, most of the major products and services of the company have actually been developed during this 20 per cent free time.

It may be a coincidence, but the reason I began to focus on global issues such as the environment, poverty and world peace was thanks to the conclusion I arrived at after investing part of my time in reflecting deeply about future concerns. My colleagues and I asked ourselves, 'Are we too focused on issues close to us? Shouldn't we be thinking more widely?' We needed to explore new paths.

Thirty years ago, I asked my colleagues to set aside their current projects to start freely exploring new issues to help decide where our efforts should be focused. After one year of significant deliberation, we were able to narrow the topics down to three prominent issues: environmental issues, at the global level; poverty in developing countries, at the pan-human level; and peace and unification on the Korean peninsula, at the national level. In addition, we agreed that at the individual level, practice was the most important thing.

Before tackling these issues in earnest, I went to a temple to reflect on the task ahead while working as a manual labourer. This gave me time to escape from my focus on current issues and explore how best to proceed.

At that time, our decision to put aside existing issues was met with criticism. However, 30 years later we are now being commended for taking a lead on environmental protection, relief aid and unification efforts.

The time and effort invested in that year of thinking recharged us and transformed our lives. It also proved that we achieve better results and see everything more clearly when we step outside our established frameworks.

When we're busy running around all day, like hamsters on a treadmill, we often feel we are working against the clock. 'Where does the time go?' we ask each other. That's why, when I suggest using part of their time on new tasks, people often retort, 'I need to support my family, and I don't even have enough time to sleep properly as it is. How will I find the time?'

In the beginning, you don't need to spare a lot of time. Start with only one hour a day and increase the time gradually. You will be able to find the time if you make up your mind to do so. You can use your free time, reduce your working hours, or decrease the amount of time you spend shopping or watching television.

If you want to experience genuine joy and happiness, you need to make your life worthwhile. Difficulties won't necessarily make you unhappy, especially if you instead reframe them as challenges to be overcome. If you feel fulfilled, you'll be happy inside despite experiencing external hardships. When you use your time the way you choose, and are able to help others at the same time, you'll feel proud and fulfilled, which will naturally make you happy.

We Can Choose to Be Happy at Any Moment

We often convince ourselves that suffering and unhappiness are inevitable. However, regardless of our external circumstances, we all have the ability to be happy, and we can all choose to be happy. Regardless of family or martial problems, health or situational issues, we have a right to be happy. However, many of us refuse that right to happiness, instead giving ourselves plenty of reasons to justify unhappiness.

I have a competitive advantage in life in that I am happier than other people. It's not because I have more skills or because I was born with more talent. Although I'm not married, I'm happier than a lot of people who are married.

I'm also happier than many people who are younger or healthier than I am.

None of us is perfect, so we all sometimes become irritated, angry, exhausted or greedy. However, regardless of our shortcomings, we should be positive and think, 'Yes, I get irritated, but I get less irritated than before. I also experience suffering, but I experience suffering less than before.'

After all, who is responsible for your happiness or unhappiness? In every situation, you are the only one who is completely responsible. No one else can share this responsibility. Even if you fail an important exam, break up with a romantic partner, or lose a loved one, you can lead a happy life. Regardless of your situation, insisting that you can't help but suffer is a waste of your life.

No matter what troubles you may face, you have the right to be happy. Use this as a guiding principle of your life. Don't hand over responsibility for your life's happiness to your partner or children, or even to a deity. Please remember that you are the one who has control over your happiness and unhappiness in your life.

Here is the Buddha's teaching on this topic:

'I am the one who creates my own happiness. I am the one who creates my own unhappiness. Nobody creates my happiness or unhappiness except for me.'

In your relationship with your country, community, or society, the same principle applies. No matter where you live, remember that you are not a guest but rather the master of your own location.

Do you think that because you're unhappy in the country where you currently live you will become happy if you emigrate? You may think that you will be happy once you live in another country, but once you arrive, you will realize that this is not the case. Likewise, students at secondary school may think their troubles will be over once they begin their new lives at university, but that is not the case either. Young people may think that their problems will be solved once they get married, but marriage brings plenty of problems of its own. Parents think they won't have anything to worry about when their children become adults, but they keep worrying even after their children leave the nest. This is the reality of human life.

We have a tendency to think, 'When I get this, I will be happy. When I attain that, I will be free.' We fervently believe this to be true, but it's far from reality. Whatever circumstances you find yourself in, you should be able to be happy and free in the here and now. Otherwise, you will find that you cannot attain that happiness or freedom you long for. There are many who just dream of happiness only to die without ever experiencing it. Instead of dreaming about happiness, you must experience it for yourself.

Set down the heavy burdens you carry and turn your eyes to other people's pain and difficulties. Volunteer several hours a week or multiple days a year; use your energy and talents to help others without expecting anything in return. When, instead of focusing on personal gain and success, we live our lives with the aim of being a person who is helpful to others and is needed in the world, we ourselves become happy while also benefiting the world. This is the way we can exercise our right to be happy.

ABOUT THE AUTHOR

Ven. Pomnyun Sunim

Ven. Pomnyun Sunim is a peace activist who delivers messages of peace and reconciliation. A humanitarian activist who provides various forms of aid to developing countries, he is a thinker who is paving the way toward a new alternative civilization, and an awakened practitioner. In 1988, he founded the Jungto Society, a community of practitioners who vowed to free themselves from suffering and devote themselves to serving others and the world by each leading the life of a bodhisattva.

Ven. Pomnyun Sunim's Dharma talks are clear and straightforward. He has an exceptional ability to explain the Buddha's teachings in simple, contemporary language. As a result, his spoken and written messages help each of his followers to redirect their gaze inward in self-reflection. The esoteric content of Buddhist sutras is brought to life thanks to his wisdom, intuition and insight.

As of January 2025, YouTube videos of Sumin's Dharma talks have had more than 1.7 billion views. He shares his wisdom about how to free oneself from suffering and how to become happy through his Dharma Q&As and the Happiness School programme. To date, he has delivered more than 12,000 Dharma Q&As in South Korea and about 300 Dharma Q&As in other countries around the world, including the 115 talks he gave during his global tour in 2014. Also, since the Covid-19 pandemic began in 2020, Ven. Pomnyun Sunim has been interacting with hundreds of thousands of people through his weekly online Dharma Q&As in Korean, and bi-weekly talks in English. (For more information, see his website: https://pomnyun.com.

Among the more than 50 books Ven. Pomnyun Sunim has published in Korean so far, the most notable are *Things Are Good as They Are Now*, *Buddha* and *Commentary on the Diamond Sutra*. His books encompass a wide range of subjects. *Words of Wisdom for Newlyweds*, *The Right to Be Happy* and *I Am a Decent Person* provide insightful advice to young people. *Lessons for Life* is a guidebook for people living in modern society. *Prayer: Letting Go* is a manual for lay practitioners. *Practice Guidebook for Teachers* imparts wisdom for teachers. *The River of Life Flows* discusses an alternative solution to the environmental problem. And *Why Is Unification Necessary?* offers a vision for peace and unification on the Korean peninsula. Some of these books have been translated into other languages, including English, French, Thai, Japanese, Chinese and Vietnamese. So far eight of these books have been translated into English, including *Awakening*, *True Freedom*, *Prayer* and *Monk's Reply to Everyday Problems* to list a few. To date, six have been translated into Chinese, three into Thai, two into Japanese, two into Vietnamese and one into French. Among the few books that were translated into multiple languages *My Happy Way to Work* was translated into Thai, Chinese, Japanese and Vietnamese, and *What Is Happiness?* is now available in English, Vietnamese and Japanese versions.

Based on the idea that practice at the individual level goes hand in hand with social engagement, Ven. Pomnyun Sunim has engaged in extensive peace initiatives for various causes, including a peaceful unification of the Korean Peninsula, refugee support, international relief efforts and interfaith reconciliation and cooperation.

Throughout the years, he has received numerous awards in recognition for his efforts. In 2002, he received the Ramon Magsaysay Award for Peace and International Understanding, and he was presented the 37th Niwano Peace Prize in 2021.